Cover illustration: *Returning to camp from a bear hunt* (see page 40).
(*Harper's Weekly,* May 29, 1875)

Cover and book design: Laurie Goralka Design

ILLUSTRATIONS OF HISTORIC COLORADO

BY CHRISTIAN J. BUYS

WESTERN REFLECTIONS, INC.

Buys, Christian J.
        Illustrations of Historic Colorado
        Included Index
        1. Colorado History I. Title

Library of Congress Catalog Number 99-066926

ISBN 1-890437-42-5

Western Reflections, Inc.
P.O. Box 710 • Ouray, CO 81427

2000

First Edition

To my brother, Ekdal J. Buys, Jr.

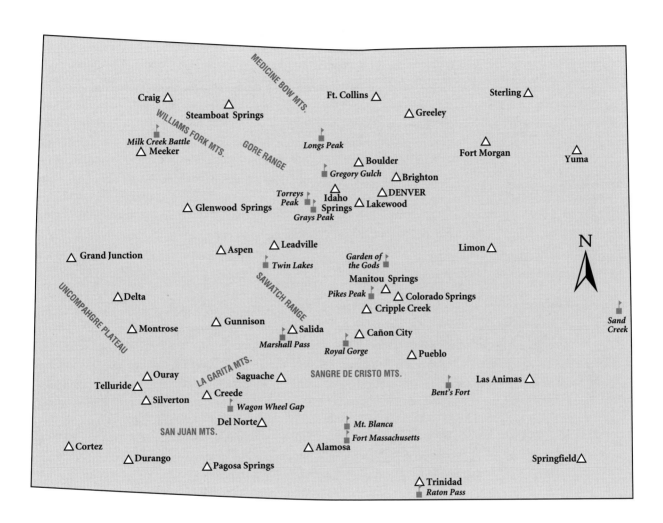

Acknowledgements

Tim Hughes graciously located many of the original illustrations reprinted in this book. P. David and Jan Smith also provided me with several drawn images. Barbara Dey in the Stephen Hart Library at the Colorado Historical Society led me to railroad surveys containing early illustrations and information related to historic Colorado. Staff members in the Western History Department at the Denver Public Library ably assisted me in locating drawings of trappers and fur traders.

A special thanks to Rita Eisenheim and Barbara Springer for their excellent editorial suggestions and to Laurie Goralka Casselberry for her exemplary art direction, design, and production. Lastly, I want to express my gratitude to P. David and Jan Smith for their unwavering support and encouragement during the course of this project.

Contents

Sixteenth-century Spanish and Mexican adventurers undoubtedly first glimpsed that portion of North America now within the boundaries of present-day Colorado. They did not stay. In the mid-nineteenth century prospectors discovered gold in the Rocky Mountains, then the rush to present-day Colorado began.

Chapter Two
Statehood and the Boom Years (1870s)

Towns blossomed throughout the new state of Colorado. Most of
them thrived because of their proximity to mining activity and the
rapidly expanding narrow-gauge railroad systems that wound their
way through the rugged foothills to the bustling mining centers.

Chapter Three
The Price of Progress (1880s - 1890s)

Colorado goes from a booming frontier state to one best by
financial crises and deadly labor strife. Yet toward the end of
the nineteenth century, gold is discovered in Cripple Creek,
the cattle industry booms, and more tourists flock to
Colorado's scenic environs.

Bibliography
Index

Entered according to the Act of Congress, in the year 1879, by FRANK LESLIE, in the Office of the Librarian of Congress at Washington.

Preface

Illustrations of early Colorado offer one a unique and fascinating glimpse into the past. They afford the opportunity to view nineteenth-century Colorado through the eyes of artists. Before the dominance of the unblinking eye of the camera, artisans bequeathed to us a treasure trove of historic images. Most of these images are skillful representations of what the artists saw. Others are fanciful embellishments. Still others are flush with social prejudice and commercial motivation. Ultimately, they all reveal something about the environment, life, and social attitudes in early Colorado.

Early in this project, I decided to let the artists, whenever possible, speak for themselves through their illustrations and their commentary. I have included original narratives from other nineteenth-century sources as well. In this way the artists and their contemporaries speak directly to us from the nineteenth century. These original chronicles offer an intriguing, albeit at times disturbing, mosaic of Coloradans' perceptions of themselves and the world around them. Further, all quotations in this book are verbatim. I used the illustrators' and authors' precise words, including misspellings, typographical errors, and grammatically incorrect sentences. I inserted "[sic]" only when the awkwardness demanded it; otherwise the large number of "[sic]" inserts would have interrupted the flow of the quotes.

It is almost impossible to comprehend the immense popularity that these illustrations enjoyed during the nineteenth century in North America. The periodicals they animated, *Harper's Weekly, Harper's Monthly, Frank Leslie's Illustrated Newspaper, Scribner's, Gleason's Pictorial,* as well as

THE·R·H·POOH·PTG·CO·CINO·

The *Illustrated London News* and others; served as people's televisions, movies, videos, and Internet all rolled into one.

Neither the artists themselves, nor the graphic technicalities of their work, are the focus of this book. Yet I admire their talents and am grateful for the images they have left us. Their skillfully crafted woodcuts, lithographs, engravings, and sketches mesmerized nineteenth-century readers. The works of gifted artisans like Albert Bierstadt, Charles Graham, Thomas Moran, Frederic Remington, Jules Tavernier, Paul Frenzeny, Winslow Homer, and Thomas Nast still garner attention in popular articles and books. Modern academicians continue to analyze and debate the effects of these images on America' s collective memory. Specific to drawings of Colorado, Clifford P. Westermier's (1970), *Colorado's First*

Portrait: Scenes by Early Artists, helped pave the way for endeavors like this one.

I have also included less prominent yet enlightening illustrations from travel guides, railroad propaganda, newspapers, business directories, promotional material for towns and resorts, and government surveys. I enjoy all the illustrations, although I favor portraits and landscapes. Portraits allow one to gaze into the souls of their subjects—the indescribable sorrow of the Native Americans, the innocence of children, the absolute assuredness of social crusaders. Landscapes exude an exotic, fresh air that makes one yearn to embark on an adventure to such untamed places. And that is how I hope you will feel as you venture into these early illustrations of Colorado.

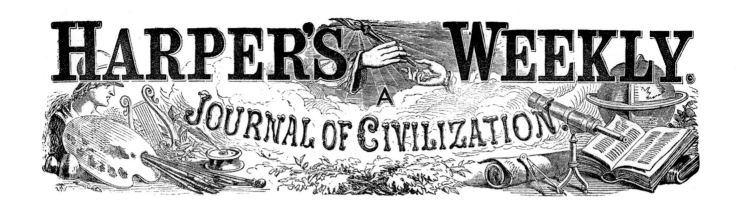

Chapter One
Before Colorado
(1850s - 1860s)

Sixteenth-century Spanish and Mexican adventurers undoubtedly first glimpsed that portion of North America now within the boundaries of present-day Colorado. They saw no — as rumored — volcanoes, woolly mammoth or blue-eyed, blond-haired people. What they did see, however, was spectacular: indescribably beautiful mountains, valleys, and deserts intersected by churning turquoise rivers. As for inhabitants, there were plenty of them; although none had blond hair and blue eyes. These sixteenth-century adventurers did not stay, because they did not find what they sought: The Seven Cities of Gold.

For the next two centuries, this faraway western region of the present-day United States saw few interlopers. Of course, ever opportunistic and paranoid European and North American powers knew it was there. As for its particular geographical features, they knew virtually nothing.

Nevertheless, geographic ignorance did not prevent them from claiming large portions of these vast "unexplored" deserts and wildernesses. With unmitigated gall, old and new-world nations vied for ownership of these huge tracts of "unoccupied" land.

When Thomas Jefferson became the third President of the nascent United States in 1801, the Mississippi River formed the western boundary of the country. In 1803, to fatten the coffers of Napoleon's war machine, France sold the region between the Mississippi River and the Rocky Mountains to the United States. It doubled the young country's size. In 1804, President Jefferson provided the inspirational impetus and money for Merriweather Lewis and George Clark to lead an expedition into this new region, then on through unclaimed Oregon country to the Pacific Ocean. Jefferson hoped that they would find a northwest water passage connecting the Atlantic to the Pacific. Lewis and Clark did not find the coveted passage, although they ultimately reached the Pacific Ocean. Two years later the group returned from this "vast uncharted wilderness" with mesmerizing tales of the things they had seen and done. The United States hailed them as national heroes. The small expeditionary force never entered the boundaries of present-day Colorado, but it opened the door to further exploration and occupation of the entire western expanse. On their way back down the Missouri River in 1806, Lewis and Clark encountered — much to their surprise — traders and trappers already heading into this immense new territory.

Almost without warning, a profound transition in the West had begun. On the heels of the old traders and trappers, thousands of gold-hungry fortune seekers in rickety wagons struggled through the Great American Desert on their way to the California goldfields. Fleeing Mormons soon deepened the wagon ruts west. Then in 1859, prospectors discovered promising gold deposits along the Eastern Slope of the rugged Rocky Mountains, near Pikes Peak and Cherry Creek. Thousands of fortune seekers who had missed the California rush flocked into the Rockies. Imagine the exhilaration of setting out to find a fortune in gold in a pristine mountain environment teeming with wildlife and boundless acres of free land. It was the frontier of all frontiers. The "American Dream" come true. There were problems, like claim-jumping and false promises of easy riches, but the undeveloped West — with present-day Colorado at its core — beckoned like never before. By the 1860s, Denver City, Blackhawk, Georgetown, and Central City sprang up almost overnight. Visions of a transcontinental railroad chugging through Denver City, Kansas Territory, started dancing in developers' heads. Surely this was the beginning of one of the finest and most romantic eras on the western frontier.

Or was it? What about the indigenous peoples who already occupied the "West?" Did they welcome this influx of foreign people into their homelands with open arms? At first they did. Several tribes embraced honorable mountain men, welcoming their trade. They began to worry, however, when thousands of whites in wagon trains starting passing through their homelands, depleting the grass, killing the game, spreading deadly diseases. Fortunately, they had written assurances from the distant "Great White Father" that no whites would ever settle on their prime hunting and camping grounds. Meanwhile, the Great White Father promised them money and trade goods for large portions of their land.

Some Indians already distrusted the "yellow-metal-crazy" whites who brought liquor, deadly diseases, and a brazen disrespect for the earth. Others did not worry. These strange-acting intruders would go away when the yellow metal ran out. Besides, they were a soft people. If necessary, they could be driven out.

Extraordinary country

The first explorers of that portion of the North American continent now embraced within the boundaries of Colorado Territory, were undoubtedly Spaniards and Mexicans — adventurers from New Spain. The first well authenticated account of the discovery of the mountain ranges, plateaus, streams, valleys and plains that form the diversified physical features of this vast Territory, is the record of Vasques Coranada, a Spanish military captain . . . . They were well armed and equipped, and commenced their explorations early in the year 1540 (Wallihan and Bigney, 1870). (Crofutt, 1881)

That useful class of mountaineers

Spanish explorers passed through present-day Colorado in search of El Dorado. Two centuries later mountain men (right) also penetrated the far reaches of the remote Rocky Mountain regions, including present-day Colorado. They sought beaver that would bring them gold. And they stayed.

The first organized expeditions to venture into the Rocky Mountains, like those headed by Zebulon M. Pike and John W. Gunnison, often depended on these romantic and restless souls for vital information. The 1853 - 1854 report of Captain Gunnison's expedition to survey a railroad route to the Pacific Ocean read: *Our recent experience in exploring a wild mountainous country without guides, was such as to show the necessity of profiting by the practical lessons in geography gained in the school of the trapper and hunter, by that useful class of mountaineers who have spent many years of their lives in encountering the hardships and imminent dangers hourly incident to their occupation in these fields of savage barbarity, short-lived gratitude and native grandeur, which are annually stained by the sacrifice of some of their numbers as victims of unbridled ferocity* (Senate Executive Document No. 78, 1855). (Denver Public Library, Western History Department)

Beaver reigned

Killing bear brought mountain men notoriety; killing beaver brought them money. In the early 1800s fashion conscious easterners craved beaver skin hats. Even the word "beaver" meant "a top hat made of beaver's underfur." Consequently, *much of the hunter's life was spent in water. In the evening twilight he waded cautiously upstream, searching out good sets for his traps. These he placed under the icy water in the beaver's natural runway, chaining each trap in such fashion that the caught animal would be drowned before it could reach land and gnaw off its paw. Over each set he bent a twig baited with evil-smelling castoreum. The next dawn he examined his line, often having to reach deep to retrieve his prey, skinned the corpses, and packed the hides back to camp* (Lavender, 1954). (Denver Public Library, Western History Department)

Fatal impact

In the 1830s trapper Osborne Russell wrote: *There seems to be a happiness in ignorance which knowledge and Science destroys here is a nation of people contented and happy they have fine horses and lodges . . . . if he [a hunter] fetches a deer at night from the hunt joy beams in the faces of his wife and children and if he returns empty a frown is not seen in the countenances of his companions* (Russell, 1965).

Then came the unscrupulous trappers' liquor. *The men threw away every possession for alcohol, their squaws were lucky to hold back a pair of second-rate robes for necessary awls, kettles, or knives — and many of the women were as drunken as the men . . . . the orgies pass civilized belief. The Indians vomited over themselves and each other, grew lecherous and broke homes with almost public adulteries, sold their daughters for a night to the traders, howled, sang, and eventually began to fight. The women whooped, squealed, and pulled hair. Often the trader [above] was endangered by the passions he unleashed* (Lavender, 1954). (Denver Public Library, Western History Department)

Beckworth reproves his Indian wife

Names like James Beckworth, Charles Bent, William Bent, Kit Carson, and Antione Robidoux, among others, have become synonymous with Colorado's colorful mountain-men era. Some of them became an integral part of the infamous fur-trading companies as well.

Some of these mountain men also felt comfortable passing between white and Indian cultures. For example, James Beckworth (above) took an Indian wife, frequently wore Indian attire, and lived in Indian villages. The caption on this illustration of Beckworth, whose multicultural background inflamed passions among other traders, reads: *Beckworth reproves his Indian wife.* (Denver Public Library, Western History Department)

The Rocky Mountain College

Solitary trappers and hunters, like the one shown above, often shared lodging during the winter months. An early trapper reminisced: *We all had snug lodges made of dressed Buffaloe skins in the center of which we built a fire and generally comprised about six men to the lodge . . . . I for one will cheerfully confess that I have derived no little benefit from the frequent arguments and debates held in what we termed The Rocky Mountain College and I doubt not but some of my comrades who considered themselves Classical Scholars have had some little added to their wisdom in these assemblies however rude they might appear* (Russell, 1965). (Denver Public Library, Western History Department)

Buffalo pelts replace beaver pelts

By the late 1840s, fickle fashion mavens in the East had declared beaver top hats bourgeois. Only silk top hats would do. The lucrative beaver pelt market collapsed. Trappers' fortunes immediately nosedived, although by the early 1840s most trappers realized that the badly depleted beaver populations would soon vanish anyway. Enterprising mountain men who wanted to stay in the West began to trade with the Indians for buffalo pelts — buffalo pelts that would make many of them rich.

The prairies of North America, west of the Mississippi, abound with vast herds of buffaloes, which form almost the entire food of many Indian nations, who have many modes of hunting down these powerful animals. One of the most characteristic is represented in the drawing [left] (*Gleason's Pictorial Drawing-Room Companion,* November 29, 1851).

Fort Massachusetts

Those following in the trappers' and traders' footsteps set up small, primitive military cantonments like Fort Massachusetts (above) to protect and aid settlers slowly filtering into the Rockies. Located in the shadows of the Spanish-named Sangre de Cristo Range, Fort Massachusetts's small garrison welcomed Captain Gunnison and his railroad surveying party in the early 1850s. (Senate Executive Document No. 78, 1855) (Colorado Historical Society, Stephen Hart Library)

The Bald-Headed Eagle

These magnificent predators frequently soared over Fort Massachusetts. *The bald eagle also destroys quadrupeds, as lambs, pigs, etc; and there are well authenticated instances of its attempting to carry off children. When the bird has fasted for some time, its appetite is extremely voracious and indiscriminate, and it will eat almost any food* (Gleason's Pictorial, June 4, 1853).

A botanical wonderland

Botanists John Torrey and Asa Gray (Torreys Peak and Grays Peak are their namesakes) accompanied Gunnison's surveying expedition that passed through Fort Massachusetts. During their arduous trek from the Mississippi River to the Pacific Ocean this duo discovered, documented, and drew numerous new plant species. Torrey and Gray seemed particularly fascinated by striking new varieties of desert cacti (above: *Echinocactus whipplei*) in present-day southwestern United States.

Grammarians would be interested to know that on June 3, 1890, the federal Board of Geographic Names dropped the possessive apostrophe from several mountain peaks, including Torreys and Grays. They reasoned that these men had never actually owned the mountains or other places named after them. (Senate Executive Document No. 78, 1856). (Colorado Historical Society, Stephen Hart Library)

Now rare in Colorado

This beautiful species of prickly pear cactus (left) also caught the attention of Torrey and Gray. It is now rare and found only in eastern Colorado.

While the expedition sought cacti, it did not seek the native peoples. Indeed, the group kept a *safe distance* from the *hostiles* whenever possible. *During the day's ride we had occasionally seen the smokes from the signal-fires of the Indians in the mountains, but they did not molest us, although we subsequently learned that a party of New Mexicans had been robbed by them, near where we saw 'smokes' just as we were passing them* (Senate Executive Document No. 78, 1855). (Colorado Historical Society, Stephen Hart Library)

Perceptions of the inhabitants

Nothing speaks clearer about the attitudes toward native peoples in the Rocky Mountains than the words used to describe them. *This brief notice of the inhabitants of Colorado will be confined entirely to the present white, or 'quasi' white, population. The aborigines of the country still occupy some of the best agricultural lands of the territory, but it is to be hoped they will soon be pushed further west or south, beyond our limits. The Indians should occupy no country which is suitable for the habitations of civilization* (Wallihan and Bigney, 1870). (Wood, 1889)

Indescribable scenery

Celebrated travelers, learned tourists, versatile newspaper correspondents, poets, authors and editors have exhausted the vocabulary of laudatory phraseology in attempting to describe the grandeur, beauty and sublimity of the mountain and valley scenery of the 'Switzerland of America,' and have acknowledged their attempts, failures. As well might we hope to achieve these things which only gods can accomplish, as to expect to portray, with our humble powers of expression, the wondrous beauty and marvelous sublimity of a view from the summit of the Rocky range . . . (Wallihan and Bigney, 1870). (Crofutt, 1881)

Artistic license

This illustration shows the camp of the artist who drew the mountain scene above. One would think that artists could have easily captured the *wondrous beauty and marvelous sublimity of a view from the summit of the Rocky Range.* All they had to do was faithfully draw what they saw. Yet many artists, including this one, attempted to embellish their drawings by adding extra ranges, changing the scale, or inserting fanciful rock outcrops with people perched on them. (Crofutt, 1881)

A European vision

This gradual and continuous progress of the European races towards the Rocky Mountains, has the solemnity of a providential event. It is like a deluge of men rising unabatedly, and daily driven onward by the hand of God (quote by De Tocqueville in Wallihan and Bigney,1870). (Crofutt, 1881)

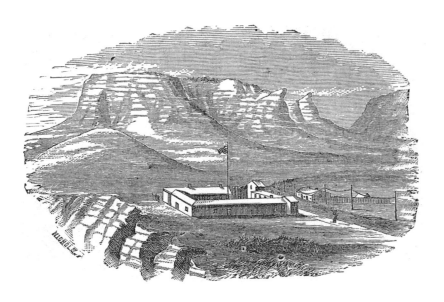

Not everyone shared the European vision

Since many western inhabitants (mistakenly labeled "Indians" by European explorers) balked at this *deluge of men* flooding into their homelands for the sake of *progress,* it was necessary to use force to ensure that this *providential event* would continue. A series of military forts constructed along emigrant routes and near new settlements backed up *the hand of God.* (Hayden, 1871) (Crofutt, 1881)

Western movie myths

Current visitors to Fort Verde Historic Park in Arizona receive a handout debunking myths created by western movies:

The Stockade: *Sand, scrub and pointed log walls, surround a desolate military post and not a tree in sight. A Hollywood myth that rewrote history . . . . Out of several hundred western military forts only about 1% ever had walls around them.*

Yellow Scarves: *Ranks of men with bright yellow scarves, neatly tied. A Hollywood costume designer[']s dream. The army never issued scarves to the soldiers. Soldiers did wear scarves, but bright colors created easy targets for the Indians.*

The Cavalry Charge: *Cavalry charging, horses at full gallop, soldiers firing their weapons rapidly. How often have you seen this? Another Hollywood myth. The carbines carried by soldiers were single shot weapons. At full gallop it was difficult to reload and fire accurately. Cavalry troopers did their serious fighting on the ground.*

The Saber: *Soldiers at full charge, sabers held high, flashing in the sun [see page 129]. It creates a striking scene, doesn't it? In real life the saber is an inconvenient weapon when the enemy has guns. It was more of a nuisance than anything. Sabers were worn for full[-]dress occasions, in garrison for dress parades, [and for] welcoming special dignitaries or high ranking officers. They were left in the barracks when the fighting started.* (*Stockades, Strikers, Bathtubs, and Other Facts*, 1998)

● In Washington with "Great Father" ●

On the opposite page is part of a *delegation, consisting altogether of eight Indians, [who] arrived in Washington . . . . to have a 'talk' with regard to a treaty made in 1861, and to have it renewed. When they sold their lands to the Government, they understood the agreement to be that they were to receive the purchase-money in hand. The United States holds the principal, however, and the Indians are regularly paid the interest.*

Three of our portraits are of Iowas, namely LAG-ER-LASH, or BRITISH, TOO-HI, or BRIER ROSE, and TAR-A-KEE, or DEER-HAM, the two first being half-civilized, while DEER-HAM represents the wild portion of the tribe. PE-TI-O-KI-MA, or HARD-FISH, is a wild representative of the Sacs and Foxes.

Some years ago one of the [delegates], *MOLESS, was sent to Kentucky, and received a very liberal English education, which, however, he failed to improve upon his return to his native wilds, and consequently he derived but little benefit from it . . . But of course enjoyment is partly the object of their visit, for an Indian considers it one of the greatest events of his life to visit Washington and see his 'Great Father.' They will also carry back with them new silver peace medals, a number of which are now being struck at the Philadelphia Mint. The medals for President JOHNSON are of full size* (Harper's Weekly, January 27, 1866).

Only crazy or very foolish men would sell their Mother Earth

The Wasichus (a 'term used to designate the white man, but having no reference to the color of his skin') went to some of the chiefs alone and got them to put their marks on the treaty. Maybe some of them did this when they were crazy from drinking the minne wakan (holy water, whiskey) the Wasichus gave them. I have heard this; I do not know. But only crazy or very foolish men would sell their Mother Earth. Sometimes I think it might have been better if we had stayed together and made them kill us all (Black Elk Speaks, 1932). (Harper's Weekly, January 27, 1866)

Mountains of Gold

Gold, the god of the avaricious — the necessity of the poor — that by its almost miraculous power transforms the fool, if its possessor, into an oracle of wisdom, or makes futile the teaching of the best, if without it, caused the foundation of this city [Denver City, Kansas Territory]. The first discovery of the precious metal was made on the Cache La Poudre, where its waters leave the mountains and enter upon the valley, by an adventurous hunting party of Cherokee Indians and Georgians. This was in the month of August, 1849. The specimens found were surface quartz, glitteringly spangled with gold, which the party on their return to the States displayed to others, thus causing small parties to venture here in search of the treasurebed.

Many small discoveries were made, but nothing of sufficient importance to create an excitement until April, 1858, when a party of traders, headed by John Cantrell, of Wesport, Mo., returned from Salt Lake, reported that they discovered rich deposits of gold on the eastern slope of the Rocky Mountains, on what is now known as 'Ralston Creek.' This report was heralded by the public prints throughout the land, and soon culminated in a wild excitement (Wharton, 1866).

Yellow metal makes Wasichus crazy

Our people knew there was yellow metal in little chunks up there [Black Hills]; but they did not bother with it, because it was not good for anything . . . . [it is] the yellow metal that makes Wasichus crazy (Black Elk Speaks, 1932).

Trains, ferries, and wagons

The year was 1859. Promoters distributed literature assuring *eastern pilgrims* of near idyllic living conditions and daily gold strikes near Denver City and Pikes Peak. In their rush to reach these Rocky Mountain El Dorados, fortune seekers used any means of transportation available. Moreover, thousands who had missed the California Gold Rush were determined to cash in on this easy bonanza. People sold their homes, businesses, and farms, then struck out across the mighty Missouri and the Great American Desert for Denver City and Pikes Peak, Kansas Territory.

For many, it did not go well. (Wallihan and Bigney,1870) (*Harper's Weekly*, 1859)

The Horrors of Travel

*T*he graphic [left] *but no means extrav-
agant illustration . . . scarcely needs any
word of explanation . . . there has come to
be a general feeling of insecurity and
distrust, and every man or woman who
steps out of a railway car or steamboat at
the termination of their journey unhurt
does so with a feeling of sensible relief
(*Harper's Weekly,* September 23, 1865).
(*Harper's Weekly,* September 23, 1865)

Not what they expected

Imagine gold-hungry pilgrims finally reaching the eastern slope of the Rockies: exhausted, famished, and desperate to sleep in a bed with a solid roof overhead in their new town surrounded by rich gold deposits. Yet this (above) is what often greeted them. As for gold, there was none to be had. Every inch of gold-bearing gravel had either been claimed or worked out. Worse, if they were lucky enough to have any money left, it went fast on the wildly exorbitant prices of food and lodging, if either was available. (*Scribner's Monthly,* August 1876)

Destitute fortune seekers

Thousands of destitute and impoverished emigrants rushed to the country in hopes of speedily acquiring a fortune. Arriving at Cherry creek, and grasping up hand-fulls of its quick-sand, and finding it not filled with the glittering wealth anticipated, they became dispirited, gloomy and embittered against the country. The destitution, suffering and hardships enduring by the returning ones in their long, weary passage over the plains, corroborated their stories (Wharton, 1866).

We hear that some of these deluded men, infuriated by the deception practiced upon them, have risen in their might, and in Denver City visited a terrible retribution upon two or *three of the prominent actors* [promoters] *in the drama. It is also reported that the conflagration of the town is threatened* (*Harper's Weekly,* August 13, 1859). (*Harper's Weekly,* August 13, 1859)

Deluded and Suffering Gold-seekers

At present date both banks of the river [South Platte] are lined with the wagons and animals of the emigrants; and the happy owners of those which have successfully 'passed over Jordan' may well cast their eyes across the swelling flood and gaze with Christian resignation upon the toiling and struggling pilgrims who have yet to prove their faith and endurance. The water rushing over the wagons, the plunging and kicking of the mules, and the imprecations of the teamsters, render the scene one of peculiar interest; and to add to it, Dog Belly, chief of the Ogallalah band of the Sioux tribe of Indians, with a small party of his braves . . . smoking the pipe of peace. Mr. Albert Bierstadt, of Boston, the artist of the expedition, is engaged in sketching their appearance. And it is to his pencil we are indebted for the illustrations [below] accompanying this article (Harper's Weekly, August 13, 1859). (Harper's Weekly, August 13, 1859)

Observations on Gold-seekers While Waiting to Cross the South Platte

During the past ten days we have met thousands of deluded and suffering gold-seekers retracing their steps to the quiet farms of the West. Many of them were in starving condition, bare-footed, ragged, and penniless; and it has caused much delay in the progress of the expedition, and materially diminished our supply of provisions to feed these hungry, home-bound strollers. We counted upon one day ninety-three wagons, and the following one eighty-four, to each of which was attached from six to ten men; and beside these hundreds of others who were wandering along without any food or mode of conveyance. Up to this point of our journey we have probably passed five thousand desponding and disappointed men returning to the States . . . (Harper's Weekly, August 13, 1859).

Ships of the plains

Once they successfully forded the South Platte, many of the well-stocked *ships of the plains* with experienced *captains* — and a little luck — made it to Denver City in reasonable shape. But crossing the great western plains was never easy. *No person can imagine how wearisome it is to travel across these plains till he has experienced it.* [sic] *we have traveled for days together with out seeing a familiar object without it* [sic] *was now and then a solitary pricklypear, which plant is a native of these desert plains. The plains are nearly bare of live grass there having been no rain of any account for sixteen months there was no water in the south platte as far as we followed it, and but little in the north platte, which was followed for near three hundred miles, while I was sick I ate nothing for nearly a week I had the yellow jaundice . . .* (quoted verbatim from a letter in Unrau, 1979). (Illustrations from *Scribner's Monthly,* August 1876)

On savoring the frontier experience

Writers and illustrators, then and now, tend to focus on the negative and unusual. Thus, early magazine articles and drawings can give the impression that nothing worked in the weird and wild West, especially for the thousands of *gold-hungry pilgrims* who turned around and went home. The burgeoning population of the West, however, including Denver City, belies such journalistic negativism. During the 1860s thousands of emigrants stayed in present-day Colorado (with more than 6,000 in Denver alone), despite the fact that there was no gold and no matter how severe the obstacles. Indeed, many of them were attracted by the pristine mountain climate, fertile foothills, and free land. And more than one pilgrim, especially while their *ships* (above) were *at anchor* in the late evening, penned words expressing their satisfaction with being part of a unique frontier experience.

Most Plains and Mountain Indians, of course, did not share this pioneer perspective. (*Scribner's Monthly,* August 1876)

For the hardy settlers remaining

The hopes of the hardy settlers remaining, who believed that immense gold fields existed in the mountains, from whence the Platte and Cherry creek received their meagre [sic] supplies of the yellow dust, waned, and had nearly died outright, when at last the sunlight of prosperity broke through the gloomy surroundings. The Gregory discovery [above] was made, and small as this now seems, in comparison to the immense deposits since found, yet it thrilled, filled, and electrified the country with pleasure. The pioneers saw and realized that their hopes were well founded, and the certain glorious prospect for the future of their adopted country, admitted no ray of doubt or downheartedness (Wharton, 1866). In less than a decade, the municipality of Central City arose around the Gregory diggings. (Hayden, 1871) (*Scribner's Monthly,* October 1879)

Central City competed with Denver City

Central CITY, Colorado, of which we give an illustration on our first page [above], is quite a large town, situated among the Rocky Mountains. It is the natural centre of the great mining operations in Colorado. Millions of dollars of Eastern capital are invested in the different mills and claims that circle the town. There has been much mismanagement on the part of Eastern agents, and this has rendered some of the best properties in the region unproductive . . . . Colorado [may become] the greatest State in the Union in its development of mineral wealth. Our artist has faithfully represented the peculiar topographical features of the mining regions among the mountains of Colorado (Harper's Weekly, February 17, 1866). (Harper's Weekly, February 17, 1866)

Elizabeth Bonduel McCourt Doe comes to Central City

Elizabeth McCourt had married Harvey Doe, a local boy, June 27, 1877, in Oshkosh [Wisconsin]. *They left soon after the wedding for Central City, Colorado. In the company of Jacob Sandelowsky she visited Leadville in December of 1879, returned to Central City, divorced Harvey, and returned to the Magic City* [Leadville] . . . (Blair, 1980). There her extraordinary beauty and charisma caught the attention of one of the most powerful and wealthy men in the West, Horace A. W. Tabor. Tabor found her charms irresistible. He divorced his wife, Augusta, and on September 30, 1882, secretly married Elizabeth Bonduel McCourt Doe, who has since come to be known throughout the world as Baby Doe Tabor.

Jacob Sandelowsky, the man Baby Doe *took up with* in Central City, used a shorter version of his name, "Sands," on his business receipts (shown below). Note the ornate "C. T." (Colorado Territory) on this early receipt. (Author's collection)

Central City, C. T. *Nov r 18 1867*

M. R. M. N. Bank

Bought of SANDS & KLINE,

WHOLESALE AND RETAIL DEALERS IN

Dry Goods, Carpets, Millinery, and House Furnishing Goods,

Main Street, opposite Post Office, CENTRAL CITY, And 216 Church Street, NEW YORK.

Dealers Supplied AT A SMALL ADVANCE ON EASTERN COST.

3¾ yds Oil Cloth — 7.50

Rec'd Pay

Sands & Kline

Another celebrated Central City citizen

Henry M. Teller (see page 81), who later became one of Colorado's most prominent national politicians, arrived in Central City in 1863. In 1865 Teller helped organize the Colorado Central Railroad and served as its president for five years. Soon Central City's optimistic residents felt they needed a first-class hotel. Teller offered to build one if the city would donate the site. The city council readily agreed. By 1872, the four-story brick Teller House (a well-worn hotel envelope is shown above) was completed at a cost of $103,000. Central City residents beamed when a year later President Ulysses S. Grant came to town and walked from his carriage into the Teller House upon a street temporarily paved with $1,300 in silver bricks. "Central" was not to be outdone by any mining town, let alone that upstart Denver. (Author's collection)

Swarming over the hills

In the early 1860s Gilpin County became the *seat of the most extensive gold mining operations in Colorado.* While Central City and Black Hawk produced most of the gold, Georgetown found itself as *the principal point . . . . [for] . . . . some remarkably rich deposits of silver ore.* Denver thrived too, although in 1863 and 1864 *many costly and useless mills were sent out from Eastern cities at great expense, and erected at the mines. . . . The new fangled machinery was not equal to saving the gold, and most of the agents sent out to superintend operations were entirely destitute of experience and knowledge necessary to make mining a success . . . . Colorado property then became perfectly dead on the market* (Saltiel and Barnett, 1868).

This economic downturn, however, did nothing to discourage hundreds of prospectors from swarming over the hills (left) in quest of more mineral riches. Ever farther and higher, they scrambled into the remote mountains and valleys of Colorado Territory. (Crofutt, 1881)

Brutal winter weather

The climate of Colorado is what an inhabitant of the temperate zone would pronounce delightful proclaimed Denver City's Business Directory in 1860. *The summer and fall is balmy and pleasant on the plains, with but few very hot and sultry days. High winds prevail, but are not of long continuance . . . Winter generally sets in late and lasts well into the spring, as much snow frequently falling in April as in any other month. In the mountains the settler can find at almost any season of the year, such a climate as he may desire, depending only on the altitude he may choose.*

Inexperienced settlers and prospectors who believed the latter portion of this promotional double-talk put their lives in jeopardy. In fact, brutal winters in the high country sent naive settlers scrambling to lower altitudes. All prospecting ceased. Incredibly, some underground mining operations — even in the 1860s — continued all winter. Daring packers (above) supplied them with food and equipment. (Crofutt, 1881)

Crossing the range on snow skates

A spectacular mountain range looms behind a solitary man descending a smooth snowfield. This crisp, sunny scene gives one the impression that it might be fun to "snow skate" across the Rockies. Not so. First, one has to ascend the mountains. Never mind the dense forests, bitter cold, deep snow, treacherous cliffs, deadly snowslides, and blinding blizzards that blow up in minutes. For most people, attempting to cross the Rockies on *snow skates* would have been tantamount to suicide. (Crofutt, 1881)

A miner's residence

Those early prospectors lucky enough to find gold in the high country pitched tents or erected small log cabins like the one shown above. *For some years, beginning with the spring of 1860, men panned the surface dirt for gold in California Gulch* [near present-day Leadville], *and when it petered out they went away* (*Harper's New Monthly Magazine*, February 1880). The writer could have added, "abandoning scores of ramshackle log cabins." Even today the remains of these crude structures can be found in remote mountain regions. (*Harper's New Monthly Magazine*, February 1880)

Returning to camp from a bear-hunt

This sketch shows a party of hunters crossing a lake in the Rocky Mountain range on their return to camp with the spoils of a successful bear-hunt. The hunters' costumes, the raft, and the bold landscape make a genre picture of the most interesting character (Harper's Weekly, May 29, 1875). More often hunters like these supplied miners with deer and elk meat. Within a few years big game became scarce near the larger mining camps. (Harper's Weekly, May 29, 1875)

PLACER MINING IN A GULCH.   PROSPECTOR WITH BURRO.

Through English eyes

Foreign correspondents flocked to the Rocky Mountain goldfields. British readers, many with relatives in America, could only fantasize about the fabulous gold strikes. *The surprising rapidity with which the mineral riches of the State of Colorado, comprising part of the Rocky Mountains range of North America, have been developed by a host of eager settlers for the past twenty years was noticed by us upon a former occasion . . . . Those who make money so easily spend it quickly, and life here tends to prodigality among all classes* (*The Illustrated London News*, May 28, 1881). (*The Illustrated London News*, May 28, 1881)

Blasting the gravel with water

When a large supply of water is at hand, and the location otherwise favorable, the 'hydraulic' system of separating gold from surface deposits presents many superior advantages. This is, in fact, the only means by which debris, containing only a trifling amount of gold, can be washed with profitable results. The apparatus for hydraulicing, consists of a strong canvas hose, from four to six inches in diameter, to which is attached a stout brass nozzle, from two to three inches in diameter. This hose must be attached to suitable pipes, which convey water from sufficient elevations to insure its forcible ejectment through the hose and nozzle. The nozzles are handled by one or two men, and the stream of water directed against the ground to be washed, and so manipulated that the washings are conducted to a proper sluice or flume, in passing through which the particles are caught in 'riffles' or retained by mercury (Wallihan and Bigney, 1870). (Crofutt, 1881)

A honey-combed mountain

This drawing shows a sight often witnessed in a rich mining country like Colorado. The hills and mountains throughout that region are literally honey-combed with tunnels, shafts, and prospecting lodes. The hardy miner is a very persevering fellow. He will turn the surface of a mountain over and over as long as there is the slightest indication of favorable results in the end. The money expended in sinking shafts and driving tunnels is very large, and often the experiment ends in complete disappointment (Harper's Weekly, July 18, 1874). (Harper's Weekly, July 18, 1874)

Reader beware

Probably drawn in the late 1860s, this eye-catching illustration appeared in *Frank Leslie's Illustrated Newspaper* in the summer of 1871 with the following caption: *Colorado, U.S. — Gulch mining at Clear Creek Canon, on the Georgetown Road, thirty miles from Denver.* A decade later, *Crofutt's Grip-Sack Guide of Colorado* (1881) printed the same illustration with the caption: *Placer mining on the San Miguel river.* That places the idyllic mining scene near Telluride, approximately 350 miles from Denver City.

The Overland Stage to Denver City

The first coach of the Leavenworth and Pikes Peak Express Company [above], *arrived in Denver on the 7th of May, 1859* (Wharton, 1866). It took them only seven days and cost the eight cramped passengers $100 each.

By the early 1860s, it seemed like all wagon and stagecoach roads led to Denver City. Of the trip, one reporter wrote: *The raids of the Indians upon parties journeying by this route across the plains have added a tragic interest to the subject* (*Harper's Weekly,* January 27, 1866). (*Harper's Weekly,* January 27, 1866)

A gaggle of artists

Artists like these bequeathed to history lasting images of the West and Colorado Territory. Many of them also wrote colorful narratives for their drawings. (*Harper's Weekly,* January 27, 1866)

Denver City, formally St. Charles, prospers

Denver is the leading town of Colorado, and lies under the very shadow of the Rocky Mountains, a few miles north of Pikes Peak. The vast trains of 'prairie schooners,' as the tented wagons seen in our sketch are called, give the place an appearance of activity. And indeed, the amount of business transacted in Denver is wonderful, when the small number of inhabitants is considered (Harper's Weekly, January 27, 1866).

The town of St. Charles was located on the site where Denver now stands, and the first cabin was built by General Wm. Larimer, in the latter part of October, 1858, and was of prevailing fashion, consisting of round logs and dirt roof. It stood on the east bank of Cherry Creek, between Blake and Wazee streets (Wharton, 1866). (Harper's Weekly, January 27, 1866)

Rag of treason

When news of the outbreak of the rebellion reached Denver, it found the people, irrespective of party, generally on the side of the Union. The exceptions to this rule were found mostly among the roughs, sports and the more ignorant class of emigrants from the Southern States.

On the 24th of April, a small rebel flag was hoisted over the store of Wallingford & Murphy, on Larimer street. The parties who thus attempted to bring disrepute upon the city, were of the characters named, and finding the popular sentiment growing too strong against them for their personal safety, soon lowered the 'rag of treason' (Wharton, 1866). (Author's collection)

Bushels of gold dust

*The banking houses are crowded with miners in all sorts of costume, bringing the bags of 'dust' to exchange for greenbacks, the dust being sold at so much per ounce. It is not an uncommon thing for bushels of gold dust to accumulate in the safes of the principal bankers (*Harper's Weekly, *January 27, 1866). The shipments of gold dust from this city [Denver City] for the sixty days previous to October 2, 1862, amounted to over one quarter of a million dollars (Wharton, 1866). (*Harper's Weekly, *January 27, 1866)*

THE **WITH**

Anatomical **Side Motion**

LEG, **AT**

THE ANKLE LIKE NATURAL ONE,

Illustrated ads

Colorado Territory's first newspapers and business directories carried several illustrated ads. The subject of these ads reflected, unfortunately for some, the needs of the readers. (Both from Wallihan and Bigney, 1870)

THE

GARDNER LEG

Comprising all the latest valuable improvements and patents.

Prices, from $75.00 to $150.00.

Warranted from 1 to 5 years.

2 TO 5 POUNDS, ONLY.

Weight, from

Cherubic figures

Winged children with chubby, rosy faces graced ads for footwear, hats, nurseries, and jewelry. (All from Wallihan and Bigney, 1870)

Shop, cor. L and Lawrence St.,   DENVER, COL.

J. M. BRUNSWICK & BROTHER,

A LARGE STOCK OF

BILLIARD TABLES

Fashionable homes and billiard tables

Contractors and builders advertised their completed products in the early *Rocky Mountain Directory and Colorado Gazetteers*. Fashionable homes soon lined Denver city streets, although it is unlikely that many respectable women played billiards, even in their own homes. (Both from Wallihan and Bigney, 1870)

At the other end of the social continuum

On Saturday, April 4th, 1860, a party of Cheyennes and Apaches visited Denver for trading purposes. During the night following their arrival, their lodges were visited by a set of drunken desperadoes, and shameless acts of violence [were] committed upon the persons of the females. The dastardly scoundrels who committed this outrage, also stole three mules belonging to the Indians, which they ran off some ten miles during the night. The Indians followed the trail next day and recovered their property. The majority of the citizens denounced the outrage, and through the efforts of Capt. James P. Beckworth, the Indians were pacified. Previous to this affair, the Indian troubles of this region had been principally on the part of the Utes, who had plundered and murdered several straggling prospectors in the mountains (Wharton, 1866). A young Ute woman (Ouray's sister) is shown above. (Frank Leslie's Illustrated Newspaper [German edition, month unknown], 1879)

Martial Law 1864

Colonel Chivington was then in command of the military district of Colorado, and, at the urgent request of the prominent business men of the city, proclaimed martial law, forbidding the opening of any houses of trade, except the dispensaries of medicines for the sick, and allowing only grocery and provision stores to be open three hours each day. All trains and wagons were prohibited from leaving the Territory. This strenuous measure was resorted to, in order to secure a sufficient enlistment of men for protection against the Indians, whose maraudings and devastation had already made the country almost uninhabitable, and who were expected in sight of the city almost every day. Every ablebodied male citizen of the city and country over the age of sixteen years, was obliged to enrol[l] himself in the militia for the common defense, and many of these were employed in the construction of block houses on the outer limits of the city, to be used as a cover in the event of attack (Wharton, 1866). When no Indian attack occurred, martial law ended, but tensions remained high.

Of these times, historian Duane Smith wrote: *Meanwhile, on the plains, cold and snow settled in, and the Cheyenne and Arapaho went into winter camps. They also had complaints: treaty agreements had not been fulfilled, settlers crisscrossed their lands, and they saw only more whites coming. Their leaders understood only too well the emerging pattern. Some of them wanted warfare, while others sought peace. The latter included Black Kettle, who took his people to a camp on Sand Creek . . . . [then] Chivington led his troops on a winter campaign . . . . and on a crisp November 29 morning, with bugles blowing, his men attacked Black Kettle's village. The officers lost control of their men . . . from that point, controversy surrounds nearly everything that happened that day — mutilations, the numbers of dead, the responsibility* (Smith, 1992).

No vindication in sight

In 1866 Wharton defended Chivington's Third Regiment attack on the peaceful Sand Creek encampment in his book, *History of the City of Denver: The exploits of this body of men, and the gallantry of their officers, will find a fair page and a clean record, in the history of Colorado. It is sufficient to state, that the regiment has been shamefully abused, for doing the very thing required at their hands — crippling the power of the most numerous and hostile tribe of the plains which Colorado had to fear, and who, without doubt, had their outrages been let go unpunished, would soon have become bold and strong enough, by being re-inforced with other hostile bands, to have massacred the citizzens* [sic] *and burned the city of Denver.*

Yet to this day, no vindication of Chivington's or his troops' behavior is in sight. Rather, the very names "Chivington" and "Sand Creek" have become synonymous with one of the most appalling acts in the history of the American West, let alone Colorado.

When the slaughter of any innocent humans, like the ones shown above, can be "justified" by any group or nation, it is time for all members of that group or nation to become gravely concerned. (*Frank Leslie's Illustrated Newspaper* [German edition, month unknown], 1879)

Blackened waste

The cry of "Fire!" in Colorado Territory's nearly all-wood tinderbox towns was perhaps the most fearsome alarm that could be spread. Even a spark in these warrens of hastily built wooden structures could ignite a fiery Armageddon. Indeed, since its inception in 1859, Denver City, like other of Colorado's early mining towns, was an conflagration waiting to happen.

The first destructive fire occurred in Auraria on the 18th of March, 1860. It was a large new frame livery stable, situated on Cherry street, between Tird [sic] and Fourth, west side. The property belonged to Messrs. Summer & Dorsett. It was entirely consumed. Loss about $18,000. Soon after, the council passed a resolution for the establishment of a

JOHN ANURE

Hook and Ladder Company and two Bucket Companies (Wharton, 1866).

Then on the morning of April 19, 1863, the "Great Fire" engulfed Denver City in flames. *The alarm was given between the hours of two and three o'clock in the morning, and in less than two hours the heart of the city was a blackened waste, the flames springing across the streets, and consuming the frame structures, rich in rosin, like tinder . . . . Thus, in two hours time, the best part of the city was reduced to ashes, and very many who had retired on the previous night, full of the comfort that independent opulence gives, awoke on the morrow impoverished and beggared* (Wharton, 1866). (*Firemen's Advocate*, July 2, 1859) (Wallihan and Bigney, 1870)

Gambling Hells of Denver

Under the rubric, *Gambling Hells of Denver*, Wharton (1866) lamented that for years gambling was *conducted in the most open and shameless manner. Large rooms [left], splendidly furnished and provided with excellent music for the allurement and enticement of the victims of the art, were kept open night and day, on the principal street of the city. At night everything that could add attraction was resorted to in order to seduce miners and strangers into the toils of the scores of blacklegs who were the habitués of these resorts. Wines, liquors and cigars of the rarest vintage and most costly brands, garnished the splendidly furnished bars, while the best musical talent of the country was employed in entertaining with vocal and instrumental melody, the crowds of customers drawn together by these allurements. Around the walls of the room were ranged the tables of the gamblers, each temptingly displaying its piles of new and shining bank notes, beside the implements of the nefarious trade, and presided over by a smiling demon, under whose blandishments there lurked a heard that considered all men his prey, and which measured humanity only by the capacity of a pocket-book and the means of getting possession of its contents.* (*Harper's Weekly,* February 17, 1866)

Chapter Two
Statehood and the Boom Years
(1870s)

In 1870 the first *Rocky Mountain Directory and Colorado Gazetteer* proclaimed:

❀ *COLORADO is just now attracting a more general and earnest attention than any other section of the new West.*

❀ *Colonies are flocking to her borders.*

❀ *Railways are girdling the continent with iron tram-ways, in the race to tap her coffers.*

❀ *Her agricultural and pastoral possibilities are unlimited.*

❀ *Her manufacturing facilities are scarcely inferior to those of factory-fostering New England.*

❀ *Her climate is delightful. Invalids here find a balm for their hurts, and healing for their disease-smitten souls.*

❀ *Poets, artists and tourists grow enthusiastic over the magnificence of her natural scenery.*

All these proclamations reeked of commercially motivated hyperbole. They were also, for the most part, true. In 1870 the Denver Pacific Railway threw open the door to Colorado Territory's majestic scenery, mineral riches, and salubrious climate. Thousands rode the rails to Denver. The mile-high city's population soared from less than 5,000 to over 35,000 by the end of the decade. Other towns, too, blossomed along the eastern foothills of the Rocky Mountains. Most of them thrived because of their proximity to mining activity and the rapidly expanding narrow-gauge railroad systems that wound their way through the rugged foothills to the bustling mining centers. On August 1, 1876, thanks to influential politicians like Jerome Chaffee and Henry Teller, Colorado finally became the thirty-eighth state in the Union. In 1877, the state's fortunes soared even higher with the discovery of rich silver deposits in the gorgeous Arkansas Valley about 120 miles west of Denver. The vortex of this frenzied mining and real estate activity took the name "Leadville." The two-mile-high "Cloud City" soon became the boom town of all mining boom towns. In 1879, the Meeker Massacre and the Battle of Milk Creek signaled the end to major armed conflicts between the settlers and the Ute Indians.

In the 1870s tourism also began in earnest. Since then, it is no exaggeration to say that Colorado has been a Mecca for tourists. At first sportsmen came with their guns, fishing poles, and tents to this land of plenty. Then came vacationers with hiking gear, eager to enjoy the bracing mountain environment. Still more people came, many permanently, in search of healthier lives in the crisp alpine air and the healing hot springs which were spread throughout this magical new state.

Historically significant dates, names, and events reveal much about Colorado's beginnings. These facts are also readily available in a plethora of excellent state history books. Original illustrations and contemporary narratives from this decade, however, reveal even more about early Colorado history. They regard academic concepts one does not normally think about: our socially conditioned perceptions and our cultural truisms. More simply put, it has to do with how Coloradans — all Americans — in the mid-nineteenth century perceived themselves and their world around them. Equally fascinating, original illustrations and contemporary

narratives reveal what Americans knew to be true — from the "inevitable progress of civilization" to the "healing powers of the nasal douche" to the "inferiority of the Indian races."

Not all the images and commentaries in this chapter are replete with socially conditioned perceptions and unexamined cultural truisms. Many are aesthetically pleasing pictorial representations of reality, accompanied by well-written, provocative historical commentary. Others betray a shocking ignorance and naivete. Still others are gross misrepresentations of reality accompanied by prejudiced commentary.

So as you turn the pages of this chapter, look carefully at each image. Listen carefully to what the illustrators and their fellow reporters had to say. Be especially wary of what the illustrators and writers *believed* to be true. Also, notice the exact words they use, the exact phrases they employ. Examine the ads and cartoons that appeared in the illustrated magazines and newspapers of the 1870s. Consider the stereotypes reinforced in Coloradans by exotic illustrations of "foreign places." Judge their medical knowledge, the treatment they sought. Reflect on their attitudes toward animals and the environment. Weigh the costs of their "immensely successful" mining industry. Ponder their perceptions of indigenous peoples. Contemplate what they valued the most in life. Finally, ask yourself if our perceptions of ourselves and the world around us differ greatly from the Coloradans of the 1870s.

Shooting Antelopes From a Railroad Train in Colorado

Shooting antelopes from the windows of a train of cars is a kind of sport only to be witnessed on the great plains of the West, and we are glad to know that it is growing into disfavor. When the trains first began running across the plains it was not unusual to stop when a large herd was near, and allow the passengers time to get out and kill as many as they could bring down. Sometimes, with the stupid curiosity that characterizes the antelope, a herd would run for miles parallel with the tracks, keeping up with the purposely slowed train, while passengers would fire at them from the car windows with rifles and revolvers. Great numbers were slaughtered — as we might say massacred — in this manner, and left to die on the plains . . . . such as . . . was witnessed by our artists near Kit Carson, Colorado (Harper's Weekly, May 29, 1875). (Harper's Weekly, May 29, 1875)

On the Iron Trail

When the railroads reached Colorado Territory in the early 1870s, people began pouring into the region. On their way across the plains they feared for their lives: *Of course, the rich booty of a train was a great temptation to the red-skins, and to capture the entire outfit, kill all the men and carry off the women, was not an unfrequent occurrence* (*Scribner's Monthly*, August 1876).

Along the "iron trails" buffalo suffered the same fate as antelope, the results of which caught the attention of one artist: *The buffalo trails stretch out over the limitless levels in crossing and converging lines. The yellow, air-cured hay of the gramma grass is not yet altogether hidden by the green spears. The dry, white beds of the water-courses, strewn with bowlders [sic], gleam at us with comfortless and voiceless sterility. The buffalo skeletons, bleached and dismembered, multiply close to the track* (*Scribner's Monthly*, August 1876). Although few could have imagined it, within two decades the great, thundering buffalo herds, over sixty million strong, had been wiped out. (*Scribner's Monthly*, August 1876)

Premonitions of Kansas

To reach Colorado, I had to go through Kansas. My premonitions of Kansas were not pleasant. My earliest recollections of the State still represent it as bleeding. I was told by an intimate and fastidious friend at Moretti's, that it raised bush-wackers and Texan cattle, that its railroad travel was liable to be interrupted at any moment by grasshoppers; and that I should have Mennonites, ranchmen, Ute Indians, army contractors and minors for society (Scribner's Monthly, August 1876). Neither did this primitive plains dwelling (above) impress the artist, but for some reason he chose to sketch it and a hog for his article. (Scribner's Monthly, August 1876)

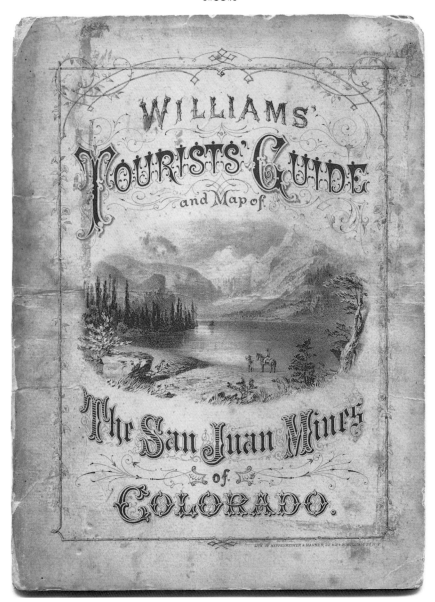

Local history and questionable enticements

Late nineteenth-century tourists' guides to Colorado usually gave a brief history of the region, followed by prolific and often questionable enticements. Shown above, *Williams' Tourists' Guide* (1877) proved no exception. First came the history: *Until September, 1872, the entire section known as 'the San Juan Country' was part of the Ute Indian reservation. At that time the Indian title was extinguished, and the country thrown open to settlement, the Indians ceding it by treaty to the government. From that period and event dates the greatest growth and development of the country, the principal development, however, having been made since the spring of 1874.* Then the enticements: [The cost of] *living is very little higher than in the plains cities. Groceries, provisions, supplies, and, in fact, everything of a purchasable character can be bought in any of the mining towns at the same price as 'at the railroad,' with cost of freight only added.* They neglected to tell the reader that the cost of freight could double the price of many items.

MOUNT OF THE HOLY CROSS.

A scene of beauty the imagination cannot depict

Many well-to-do tourists and adventurers rode the rails to Colorado solely to see the Rocky Mountains. Today that sounds fun and romantic. Back then, for many naive sojourners, it was neither. Uncomfortable and unmercifully long trains rides pummeled them. Harsh weather and "thin" mountain air exhausted them. Ribald towns bereft of common decency and law shocked them.

At least the tourists' guides could not exaggerate the mountains' beauty, no matter how hard they tried. *The undulating mass of mountains as you look upon them from higher peaks; the grand old peaks themselves, many of them hoary and snow-capped all the year; the sky itself, which seems bluer viewed through this mountain air, and the dark forests of evergreen — all combine to make a scene of beauty the imagination cannot depict* (*Williams' Tourists' Guide*, 1877). (Both from South Park railroad booklet)

MT. HARVARD FROM PARK RANGE.

TWIN LAKES.

A panacea for *out of tone* systems

To the lover of nature, or he who desires a season of rest from the cares of business, or whose 'system is out of tone,' a summer's camp out [in the Rockies] is recommended. He will win back health and vigor, refresh his soul as well, and return with broader views of human nature, as well as of his country and its great resources (Williams' Tourists' Guide, 1877). (South Park railroad booklet)

Men who fish not for sport

Fishing, for trout, is good in all streams where the concentrating works and smelters, or the saw-mill have not driven them away . . . . The tourist, pleasure-seeker, or prospector can keep his larder well supplied, in season, with the result of a brief use of the rod and line (Williams' Tourists' Guide, 1877).

In 1873, English adventurer Isabella Bird witnessed winter fishing in Estes Park (shown above in summer). *The winter fishing is very rich. In the hardest frost, men who fish not for sport, but gain, take their axes and camping blankets, and go up to the hard-frozen waters which lie in fifty places around the park . . . hack a hole in the ice . . . bait the hook with maggots . . . [and] trout are caught as fast as the hook can be baited . . . . Sometimes two men bring home 60lbs of trout as the result of one day's winter fishing* (Bird, 1873). (Scribner's Monthly, August 1876) (Crofutt, 1881)

Standard temptations

*L*ying *behind it* [Garden of the Gods] *is the main range of the Rocky Mountains, which offers all kinds of game to the sportsman. Excellent brook trout, ptarmigan or Rocky Mountain quail* [above], *red-tail deer, and ducks, snipe and grouse, to say nothing of antelopes and occasional cinnamon bear, are the standard temptations* (Scribner's Monthly, *August 1876). (*Scribner's Monthly, *August 1876)*

Yelp of a soul in another world

The very silence of the place [Garden of the Gods] *was sepulchral, and connected it with the ruin of ages. The ponderous shadow of the great wall only served, where its masses fell, to intensify the lurking objects within its limit. The melancholy bark of a coyote far up the mountain, sounded like the yelp of a soul in another world* (Scribner's Monthly, August 1876). (*Scribner's Monthly*, August 1876)

No mention of the wolverine

The artist who drew the coyote with the other-worldly yelp made no mention of an encounter with a wolverine, although this illustration appeared in the same article. Surely the wolverine fell in the *standard temptation category* as well. (*Scribner's Monthly*, August 1876)

A Colorado Tragedy

In 1874 Colorado Territory became known for more than its mountains, mines, and recreational opportunities. Cannibalism reared its heinous head. *Ouray, chief of the Utes, advised the [Packer] party not to proceed across the mountains, as it was very dangerous at that time of the year on account of the snow, but to remain at his camp until spring when the route would be open. They did not heed Ouray's warnings. On the 9th of February a party of six . . . left the Indian camp for the Los Piños agency, which they were informed was about seventy-five miles distant. They had ten days' provisions, and were packed out thirty miles on horses by the Indians.*

Packer arrived at the agency alone, having been out sixty-five days. On being questioned as to the whereabouts of his comrades, he said he was the only survivor, the others having died or been killed, and their bodies eaten. His story was that the old man Swan, being sickly and weak, was the first to succumb to the hardships of the march, and that his dead body was eaten by his surviving companions. The next victims were . . . killed accidentally, according to Packer's story. Of the three surviving men, two were armed with guns . . . . these two killed and ate their unarmed comrade (Harper's Weekly, October 17, 1874). (Top and bottom illustrations from *Harper's Weekly*, October 17, 1874) (Center illustration from *Frank Leslie's Illustrated Newspaper*, November 8, 1879)

An artist makes a grisly discovery

The fate of the missing men remained a mystery for several months, until the accidental discovery of the camp where the bodies were lying. In the latter part of last August Mr. John A Randolph, an artist, who was out on a sketching tour in the Uncompahgre Mountains, was startled one afternoon by coming suddenly upon the remains of five human beings. They were lying in a gloomy, secluded spot, densely shaded by tall trees . . . marks of violence on each body indicated that a most terrible crime had been committed. There had been no attempt to conceal the remains. No guns or camping utensils were found with them, nor a trace of any boots or shoes . . . . The coroner of Hinsdale County, Colorado, in which the bodies were lying, was immediately notified (Harper's Weekly, October 17, 1874).

Eventually Packer confessed cannibalism and was convicted of murder, a sentence that was later reversed by the Colorado Supreme Court. Paroled in 1901, he died in 1907 and was buried in Littleton, Colorado. Researchers continue to debate the legitimacy of the evidence and the merit of the man. (*Harper's Weekly*, October 17, 1874)

Denver, *the great braggart city*

In 1873 English horsewoman Isabella Bird described her ride into Denver: *The windy cold became intense, and for the next eleven miles I rode a race with the coming storm. At the top of every prairie roll I expected to see Denver, but it was not till nearly five that from a considerable height I looked down upon the great 'City of the Plains,' the metropolis of the Territories. There the great braggart city lay spread out, brown and treeless, upon the brown and treeless plain, which seemed to nourish nothing but wormwood and the Spanish bayonet* (Bird, 1873).

By the time the artist drew this panorama of Denver in the mid-1880s, it had more trees, buildings, and people. The 1870 census listed Denver's population as 4,759. By the 1880 census it had soared to 35,718. A few other Colorado cities, including Central City and the mighty Leadville, would challenge Denver for supremacy. But *the great braggart city* remained supreme in the state. (Ingersoll, 1885)

Cities blossomed along the eastern slope of the Rockies

Fort Collins, Cañon City, Colorado Springs, and Pueblo all blossomed in the 1870s. To the south, Pueblo boasted tree-lined residential streets (above) and the finest county buildings in the state. Its smelters, mills, and foundries fueled the local economy, but darkened the skies above the city. *Pueblo is the centre for a vast extent of agricultural, stock-raising, and mining country, and for its size* [approximately 3,500], *does an immense business, but sadly needs a 'good' hotel* (Crofutt, 1881). (*Scribner's Monthly,* August 1876)

High fashion in Denver

The more fashion conscious in the frontier city tried to keep abreast of the latest trends in the East and Europe. L. Garson and Company on the corner of 15th and Holladay offered stylish overcoats for boys (right). Denver's social mavens swooned over the stunning hat (opposite page) drawn in *Harper's Weekly*. (*The Denver Daily Tribune*, November 16, 1876) (*Harper's Weekly*, May 29, 1875)

Statehood in 1876

*T*he Territory of Colorado, which was prevented by Andrew Johnson from entering the Union in 1866, was now after the lapse of ten years, admitted as a State under a bill approved by General Grant in the closing year of his Presidency. The Territory had in the long interval developed great wealth in the precious metals, in rich deposits of iron and coal, and most surprising of all, in its agricultural resources. The two senators, Jerome B. Chaffee and Henry M. Teller, were kinsmen and were among the pioneers of the Territory who had been deeply concerned in it is progress and development. Mr. Chaffee had represented the Territory in Congress for the six years immediately preceding its admission as a State, and had worked with energy and success for the interest of his constituents He was somewhat impaired in health when he took his seat in the Senate, and did not desire to remain in public life. Mr. Teller continued in the Senate for a longer period, and acquired political leadership in the Senate (Blaine, 1886). The new state's seal strove to include symbols for all that comprised Colorado, except the indigenous peoples. (Chicago and Northwestern Railway Company stock certificate)

William Henry Teller, Colorado's first senator

A portrait of William Henry Teller captures the eminent man's stern, honest, and uncompromising character. It is strange how so little notoriety has accrued to Teller. He took his seat in the United States Senate on December 4, 1876. During his thirty-three year stint in Washington, D. C., he found himself at the center of several rancorous issues: bimetallism (a silver and gold-based monetary system), the "re-education" of American Indians, and Cuba's status after the Spanish-American War. Coloradans championed him, easterners reviled him, Indians feared him, and Cubans loved him. He also served as Secretary of the Interior (1882 - 1885) under President Chester A. Arthur. There was, however, one constant in Teller's incredible political career: everyone knew where he stood on each issue he tackled. (*National Republican: Senatorial Edition*, 1886)

Teller for President

The inside cover of a diary of Senator Teller's son reflects his nomination for United States President on the Silver Republican ticket, although he neither officially pursued nor accepted the nomination. (Glue has leached through the silk ribbon.) (Author's collection)

The parting of ways over bimetallism

Henry Teller and the political climate of his times resulted in numerous newspaper cartoons. Teller's dramatic exodus from the Republican National Convention of 1896 prompted this front-page treatment in the *Rocky Mountain News.* Teller believed that *there can be no proper financial system in any country in the world that does not recognize this principle of bimetallism.* Most of his Republican colleagues disagreed.

No issue since slavery so polarized two large segments of America. But this time it was the West, which favored both gold and silver ("bimetallism"), against the East, which championed gold (the "gold standard"). Colorado had vast reserves of both gold and silver, and thus the argument over bimetallism was particularly intense in this state. In the heat of the moment, Teller pronounced: *I believe the whole welfare of my race is dependent upon a rightful solution of this question; that the morality, the civilization — nay the very religion — of my country is at stake in this contest* [over bimetallism]. (*Rocky Mountain News,* June 21, 1896)

Illustrated Interviews with Eminent Public Men on Leading Topics of the Day

Here an *artistic correspondent* interviews the Honorable John Sherman, Secretary of the Treasury *on the financial condition of the country.* Denver bankers and business people, whose financial fortunes often depended on United States's fiscal policy and "eastern money," devoured articles like this one in *Frank Leslie's Illustrated Newspaper* (November 8, 1879). Along with local newspapers, illustrated magazines served as Denver residents' main source of financial news, and most other news. These magazines constituted their television, radio, VCR, and Internet all rolled into one. Consequently, an articulate writer and talented illustrator could wield tremendous political clout.

Political cartoons

Political cartoonists skewered many a politician. This cartoon focused on the hotly debated silver issue (see page 82). As previously mentioned, easterners championed the gold standard, while Coloradans strongly favored bimetallism, meaning they wanted both silver and gold to back the country's legal tender. Since the young state produced large amounts of both gold and silver, issues related to federal fiscal standards garnered considerable attention throughout Colorado. A severe depression in the early 1870s that sent the economy reeling further increased interest in normally boring and arcane fiscal policy. (*Frank Leslie's Illustrated Newspaper,* June 14, 1879)

Windows into their world, and beyond

The next seven illustrations reveal how periodicals provided frontier Coloradans with a window into their world, and beyond. Those who loved theatre could see and read about famous New York opera stars: *Paola Marie'* (above) *has become a favorite of New York from the first night, as she was already of Paris. Her singing and acting . . . are agreed on all hands to be revelations of wonders and novel effects in dramatic and lyric elaboration* (Frank Leslie's *Illustrated Newspaper,* November 8, 1879).

The citizens of Denver are especially a threatre-going and amusement-loving people. The old Denver Theatre is an honored, and if anything in this new country may be so termed, ancient institution (Wallihan and Bigney, 1870). (*Frank Leslie's Illustrated Newspaper,* November 8, 1879)

TENNESSEE — ARREST OF YELLOW FEVER REFUGEES BY THE SAFETY-PATROL OF MEMPHIS.

Reason to worry

All Colorado citizens feared deadly yellow fever. The sight of this sinister illustration on the cover of *Frank Leslie's Illustrated Newspaper* (August 23, 1879) sent chills up and down the readers' spines, no matter how far away from Memphis, Tennessee. Cities infested with this lethal, fast-spreading disease imposed strict quarantines [above] on all those afflicted.

Egyptian mummies in Kentucky

Imagine Egyptian mummies being discovered in Kentucky. *The wonderful caves of Kentucky — as famous as the Pyramids of Egypt — are located . . . ninety miles south of Louisville. In June, 1878, when Mr. J. R. Puckett and a few other daring explorers penetrated its mysteries by crawling several hundred yards between fallen rocks and then emerging in an avenue at least sixty feet wide. Following it for about a mile, they discovered an immense room . . . . It is called the Crystal Chamber . . . . At a distance of about three miles, in a very picturesque spot, six mummies were found on a ledge of rocks. They were reposing in stone coffins rudely constructed, and*

presented every appearance of the Egyptian mummies. Three of the mummies were male and three of them female. Mr. W. Edwin Mortimer, who resides at No. 299 Floyd Street, Louisville, Ky., purchased two of them; Mr. J. R. Puckett, a capitalist of Glasgow Junction, purchased two, and Joseph Mulhattan the remaining two. Our illustrations are furnished by the latter gentleman (Frank Leslie's Illustrated Newspaper, June 7, 1879). (Frank Leslie's Illustrated Newspaper, June 7, 1879)

Pictorial Spirit of the Illustrated Foreign Press

The promise of a better life spiced with the appeal of adventure in a new land attracted many people to Colorado. Once they settled into daily living routines, their sense of adventure did not subside. Their fascination with exotic cultures and animals remained strong, causing them to turn to a section in *Frank Leslie's Illustrated Newspaper* entitled, *'The Pictorial Spirit of the Illustrated Foreign Press.'* Scenes of battling Zulus, lumbering elephants, and bizarre Buddhas fueled their stereotypes of foreign places and travel fantasies. (*Frank Leslie's Illustrated Newspaper,* June 7, 1879)

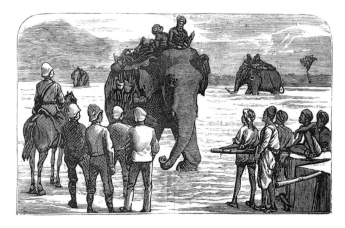

E. F. HALLACK,

DEALER IN

LUMBER, SASH, DOORS

Blinds, Mouldings, Turnings,

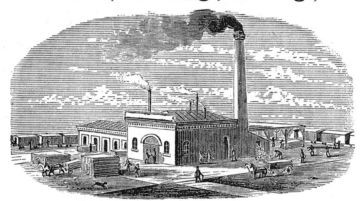

PAINTS, OILS, GLASS & PUTTY
Holladay Street, bet. I and K, DENVER.

Denver's city scene

In 1873 Isabella Bird described the mile-high city: *Denver is no longer the Denver of Hepworth Dixon. A shooting affray in the street is as rare as in Liverpool, and one no longer sees men dangling to the lamp-posts when one looks out in the morning! It is a busy place, the 'entrepot' and distributing point for an immense district with shops, some factories, fair hotels, and the usual deformities and refinements of civilization. Peltry shops abound, and sportsman, hunter, miner, teamster, emigrant, can be completely rigged out at fifty different stores* (Bird, 1873). (Wallihan and Bigney, 1870)

Denver's religious scene

The pioneers of this land of grains of gold and golden grains, though remote from the great centres[sic] of christianity and civilization, have ever been mindful of the importance of religious influences and teachings (Wallihan and Bigney, 1870). By 1878 the Presbyterians boasted a monthly illustrated newspaper, *The Rocky Mountain Presbyterian.* Drawings promoting their *Ladies' Home Missionary Society and Home Mission Band* appeared in the August 1878 issue (above and right).

Don't' drink the water

By the 1870s no one who hoped to stay healthy drank from rivers or streams near Denver. Even in the foothills one had to be cautious. Wise locals keep a sharp eye out for signs of upstream mining, outhouses, and domestic animals. (*Scribner's Monthly,* August 1876)

WESTERN BANK NOTE & ENG.CO. CHICAGO.

For those who did get sick

For the ill there was *The People's Common Sense Medical Adviser in Plain English; or, Medicine Simplified*, by R. V. Pierce, M.D. (above), *'Counselor-in-chief of the Board of Physicians and Surgeons, at the World's Dispensary.'* Published in 1875, this 888-page illustrated medical tome probably sat on many bookshelves, including doctors', in frontier Colorado. The eminent Dr. Pierce offered copious notes, or so it seemed, on every nuiance of the body's physiology, general medicine, and medicinal and nonmedicinal cures. (Pierce, 1875)

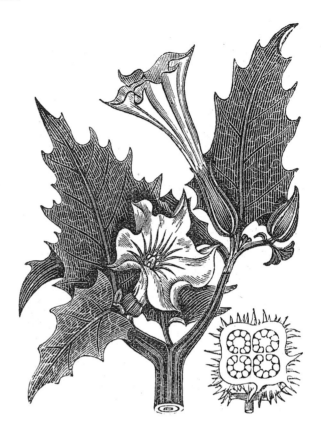

Stramonium
(Datura Stramonium)

Also known as Thorn-Apple, in large doses is a powerful narcotic poison. In medicinal doses it acts as an anodyne and antispasmodic. Dose — Of extract of leaves, from one-half to one grain; fluid extract, from three to six drops (Pierce, 1875). (Pierce, 1875)

Blood-Root
(Sanguinaria Canadensis)

Also known as Red Puccoon. Part used — the root. In minute doses Blood-Root is a valuable alternative, acting up the biliary secretion, improving the circulation and nutrition. Dose — Of powdered root, one-fourth to one-half grain; of tincture, one to two drops; fluid extract, one-half to one drop. When given in fluid form it should be well diluted (Pierce, 1875). (Pierce, 1875)

A nasal douche for catarrh sufferers

Now, in order to be most successful in curing catarrh, it is necessary that the remedy should reach and be thoroughly applied to the affected parts. This can be accomplished in only one way, which is by hydrostatic pressure. The anatomy of the nasal passages, and the various chambers and tubes that communicate therewith, is such that they cannot be reached with fluid administered with any kind of a syringe, inhaling tube or instrument, except one constructed to apply it upon the principle above stated. Such an instrument is the Nasal Douche (Pierce, 1875). (Pierce, 1875)

Colorado's *reconstructed invalids* could order direct from Dr. Pierce's *World's Dispensary*

So much has been said of the wonderful effects of a residence in Colorado in restoring invalids to health, and, in particular, of her wide-spread celebrity in the relief and cure of tubercular and pulmonary affections that a brief consideration of this important subject will not be out of place. Probably it is not amiss to assert that at least one-third of the present population of Colorado consists of reconstructed invalids. They have come here from all sections of America, and some, even, from the old world — all in eager search of the fabled Fountain . . . . Many, it must be said, came to [sic] late to be benfited [sic], and only to be buried in the land of strangers, or expressed back to their friends, in metallic caskets (Wallihan and Bigney, 1870).

Thousands of *medically distressed* Coloradans who needed more than the *healing healthful climate* to survive could order medical products, including *medicinal herb powders and the Nasal Douche*, directly from Dr. Pierce's *World's Dispensary* business (above) in Chicago, Illinois. (Both from Pierce, 1875)

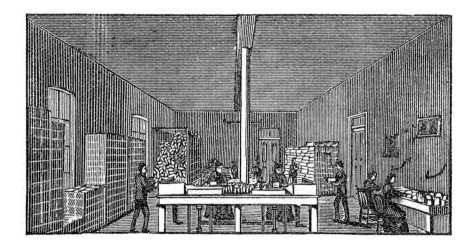

Denver Pacific Railway!

OPEN ᴛᴏ DENVER!

Connecting with UNION PACIFIC RAILROAD at Cheyenne for all points East and West.

At Denver with the Kansas Pacific Railway, for all points in the East; with Colorado Central Railroad, for Golden City, Black Hawk, and Central City; with Colorado Stage Co.'s lines, to Idaho Springs, Georgetown, Nevada, South Park, Buckskin, and Fairplay; and with Barlow, Sanderson & Co.'s Denver and Santa Fe Stage line, via Colorado City and Pueblo.

At Hughes' Station, on Denver Pacific Railway, with the Denver & Boulder Valley Railway, for Erie, Valmont, Burlington, Boulder City, and Cariboo Mines.

The Denver Pacific Railway

Through the medium of this railroad Colorado first had direct communication with all business centres, east and west; her mineral and agricultural products found a suitable market, at small expense and with trifling delay; and capitalists, tourists, and all classes of immigrants, were enabled to avail themselves of her unbounded resources, without the exposure and delay consequent upon a journey across the great plains in a stage-coach or wagon train (Wallihan and Bigney, 1870). (Wallihan and Bigney, 1870)

Wagon roads beyond Denver

Railroads reigned on the plains. Beyond Denver, wagon roads wound through the mountains. *The expense of road making on the plains is comparatively trifling; but on the mountains, thousands of dollars are often required to construct a few miles of road, as almost insurmountable barriers must be over come . . . . mountain roads are built and kept in repair almost exclusively by individuals or companies, who remunerate themselves by tolls collected from all classes of travelers* (Wallihan and Bigney, 1870). (Wallihan and Bigney, 1870) (*Scribner's Monthly,* October 1879)

Hardships of Travel in Colorado

The scene of the illustrations on this page [opposite] *lies near the eastern border of the Middle Park, Colorado, which is walled in by the Front or Snowy Range of the Rocky Mountains on the east, and on the west by the Park Mountains. It embraces a territory of about 3000 square miles, and contains the famous hot sulphur springs, whose medicinal qualities have attracted many tourists and invalids to that region. Georgetown, whence the travellers in our sketch set forth, is a thriving mining town, situated on the Front Range, at an altitude of 8412 feet, about seven miles from Gray's Peak. It derives its prosperity from the working of silver mines in the vicinity, which are thought to be practically inexhaustible. It possesses a national bank, a daily and weekly newspaper, four churches, and a number of fine hotels, besides large reduction works.*

The Argentine Pass, so formidable to pedestrians with tender feet, is a depression in the Front Range about 13,000 feet high. Two miles from the pass rises Gray's Peak to the height of more than 14,000 feet, its sides covered with forest of large evergreen trees, chiefly Douglas spruce and yellow pine.

Travel in the mountain wilds of Colorado is not what would be called a luxury, whether one goes for business or sport. The roads, or rather trails, are in the most primitive condition, and many are the hardships which the pedestrian most undergo before he finds himself at the rude way-side inn, where he can pull off his boots, indulge in a good wash, and refresh the inner man with a substantial meal (Harper's Weekly, *September 3, 1881).* (Harper's Weekly, *September 3, 1881)*

From Georgetown to Toll Gate

$10 FINE FOR PASSING WITHOUT PAYING

Toll Gate.

Topping the Agentine Pass

Bad Travelling For Tenderfeet

On the road to Leadville, boom town of boom towns

Once the word of the silver strike in California Gulch (near present-day Leadville about 120 miles west of Denver) got out, it spread immediately throughout Colorado and beyond. By 1877 the rush was on. It proved to be one of the richest, longest-lived, bawdiest phenomenon that America has ever witnessed. Thousands upon thousands of miners and entrepreneurs of almost every description and ethical inclination transformed a large portion of the pristine Arkansas Valley into what looked like a giant gopher colony. Massive stands of trees became seas of stumps. Hundreds of tents, cabins, and ramshackle buildings seemingly sprung up overnight and everywhere. Hoards of fortune seekers jammed the muddy streets and paths twenty-four hours a day. Everyone in America — or so it seemed — wanted a piece of the action. After all, this was Leadville. This was the boom town of boom towns.

On the road to Leadville, frenetic Webster Station (above) *at the terminus of the Denver, South Park and Pacific Railroad presented many 'bizarre' and picturesque sights. The pin-clad bluffs, the rude station, the stages packed full as sardine-boxes, the teams, the wagons, the newly-arrived silver-seekers panting to push on at any cost and in any mode, the freight, the successful miners returning to civilization, the haggard questioners, the yelling freighter, the bustle, hurry, turmoil, and excitement, and the thousand and one 'bits of color' . . . . Leadville will, in the immediate future, be struck by three lines of railroad, and the experienced people say that there is silver for all who may elect to travel by them (Frank Leslie's Illustrated Newspaper,* June 21, 1879). (*Frank Leslie's Illustrated Newspaper,* June 21, 1879)

To our utter and total annihilation

To reach Leadville from Denver, many people chose to negotiate the 13,000-foot Mosquito Pass — impossible in the winter and what life insurance companies called "extra hazardous" in the summer. Hauling heavy equipment over the treacherous trail exacted a terrible toll on animals and men. Nevertheless, soon Mosquito Pass *that but a year before had been almost desolate in its loneliness, was lined with a straggling stream of humanity, with their faces set toward the new El Dorado* (*Frank Leslie's Illustrated Newspaper,* April 12, 1879).

One pilgrim observed: *I have done a good deal of mountain traveling, both in this country and in Europe, and never had so much as a nerve wrung; but during my passage upwards to Leadville there were moments when my heart beat backwards as the vehicle lurched over a yawing precipice of fathomless depth . . . . and should a trace, or strap, or bolt yield, down would inevitably thunder the iron avalanche to our utter and total annihilation* (*Frank Leslie's Illustrated Newspaper,* April 12, 1879). (*Frank Leslie's Illustrated Newspaper,* April 12, 1978)

Terror of the tourists

The Road-agent is still the terror of the tourists in some of the remote Western Territories where the stage-coach affords the only means of transportation of lines of public travel . . . . The road-agent usually appears when he is least expected, and sometimes he ventures surprisingly near the borders of civilization. Thus, on a recent occasion, a stage plying between Leadville and an outlying town was stopped by two agents in the suburbs of the former city, and the passengers deliberately plundered. The process was of the usual regulation sort. While one of the men covered the driver with a revolver, the other ordered the passengers to dismount. They did so, and being arranged in a row, one road agent menaced them with a pistol, while the other relieved them of their valuables, amounting to over $2,000. Of course the robbers escaped (Frank Leslie's Illustrated Newspaper, November 11, 1882). (Frank Leslie's Newspaper, November 11, 1882)

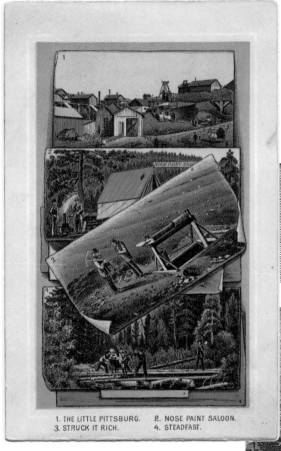

1. THE LITTLE PITTSBURG.   2. NOSE PAINT SALOON.
3. STRUCK IT RICH.   4. STEADFAST.

The two-mile-high "Cloud City"

Many contemporaries roundly condemned Leadville as a den of iniquity and a pestilence that bowed only before its demigods: sex, liquor, gambling, and avarice. Others lavishly praised the "Cloud City" as being a living monument to the American dream, where anyone, either through hard work or pure luck, could become fabulously rich. Based upon the thousands of eager immigrants from throughout the United States and Europe who flocked to Leadville, one might conclude that there was merit in both views. (Inset: South Park railroad booklet) (Crofutt, 1881)

Leadville in *The Illustrated London News*

SACUACHE RANGE.

MINES ON FRYER HILL.

PLACER MINING IN A GULCH.

PROSPECTOR WITH BURRO.

ON THE ROAD TO LEADVILLE.

TENDERFEET.

Leadville . . . . *is situated in an almost level plain, on the banks of California Gulch, four miles from its junction with the Arkansas river. This place was first explored for gold in the summer of 1860, and a camp of five thousand men had assembled here in the following years. Gold was obtained, before the close of 1865, to the amount of three our four millions sterling in value, but the yield soon afterwards declined . . . . The discovery of carbonate of lead, containing a large proportion of silver, was made at a later date, and it was not till April, 1877, that smelting furnaces treatment of this ore were erected on the site of Leadville, where a busy town of 20,000 inhabitants has since grown up. Hundreds came that year, and thousands in the year following; lines of stage-coach traffic and freight wagons, to and from Denver and South Park, were speedily established, and Leadville soon possessed its hotels, stores, banks, dancing-saloons and gambling-saloons, two or three newspapers, also two churches and a schoolhouse, for the needs or desires of a large population. The Iron Lode, the Camp Bird, the Argentine, the Carbonate, the Long and Derry, but especially that of Fryer Hill, have produced silver to an enormous amount, rivalling the great Comstock lode in the Sierra Nevada of California . . . . It is declared by some visitors to be 'the liveliest town the world can show to-day' After nightfall, by lamplight, they say, 'it fairly booms with excitement and life.' The miners then drift into town in swarms; a dozen bands are drumming up audiences for theatres and variety shows; scores of saloons and gaming-houses are in full blast, and the entire place has the aspect of a grand holiday* (The Illustrated London News, May 28, 1881). (*The Illustrated London News, May 28, 1879*)

The seventh wonder of the world

The excitement in Denver having risen to white heat, I resolved upon a visit to Leadville. The time to see this seventh wonder of the world at its best is from Saturday afternoon to Monday morning, when the miners swarm in the streets, having come in from the mountains to spend their eighteen or twenty dollars per man at faro, or in the saloons . . . . There is not a foot of ground within four miles of Leadville, in the direction where ore has been found that is not taken up. The region is one of extraordinary richness (Frank Leslie's Illustrated Newspaper, April 12, 1879). (Frank Leslie's Illustrated Newspaper, April 12, 1879)

Of the color and consistency of thick pea-soup

A very remarkable sight in Chestnut Street, Leadville, during the prevalence of a thaw. The sidewalks are thronged till locomotion save at a snail's pace is rendered impossible, since the sidewalk with its irregular planks is a sort of raft, floating high above the yellow-brown ooze — of the color and consistency of thick pea-soup — that, eighteen inches deep, incumbers [sic] the roadway (Frank Leslie's Illustrated Newspaper, June 14, 1879). (Frank Leslie's Illustrated Newspaper, June 14, 1879)

A *swell* arrives in Leadville

A few days since I was intensely amused by the sensation created by a full-blown white-shirted swell — the miners always 'go' for a white shirt — who strutted through the streets of Leadville as though he were the owner of the Prospect Mine itself. This 'nice young man' was attired after the most approved style of the 'masher' and carried his valise in so gingerly a manner as to beget the open derision of such miners as happened to be around at the time (Frank Leslie's Illustrated Newspaper, June 7, 1879). (Frank Leslie's Illustrated Newspaper, June 7, 1879)

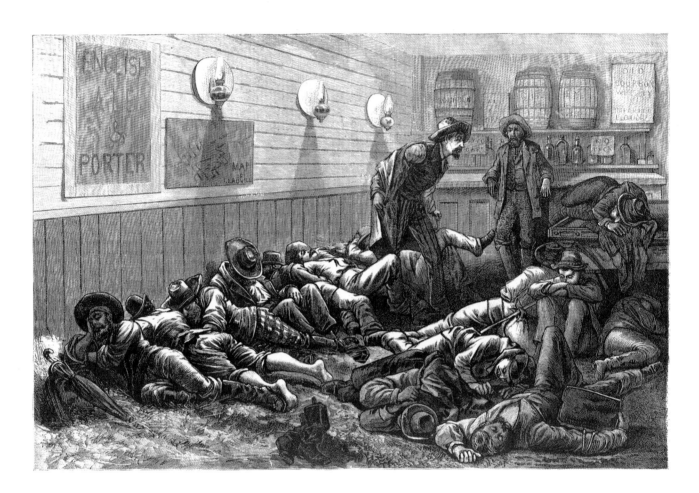

For the privilege of lying on a dirty mattress

In Leadville, there were not sleeping accommodations for those who thronged into the camp. For the privilege of lying on a dirty mattress, laid upon the floor of a boarding tent, with a suspicious blanket for a cover, and the chances of proximity to a thief or desperado, those who could afford it paid a dollar (Dill, 1881). (Frank Leslie's Illustrated Newspaper, June 7, 1879)

Contrasts of Life in Leadville, Colorado

Although Leadville is a very young town, it has already in full operation two evidences of modern civilization, generally supposed to be antagonistic in their influence — the gambling-hell [above] *and the church* [below] (*Frank Leslie's Illustrated Newspaper*, May 17, 1879). (*Frank Leslie's Illustrated Newspaper*, May 17, 1879)

Into the abyss

Illustrators relished the opportunity to describe their perilous descents into the bowels of the earth in the Leadville Mining District. *Understand that there is just about room for the bucket in the shaft, that the latter is slightly inclined, and that you catch and jar and shake in a nerve-trying way; and understand, further, that a person should carefully study his temperament and possible disabilities before he takes a contract to go into a deep shaft* (*Harper's New Monthly Magazine,* February 1880). (*Harper's New Monthly Magazine,* February 1880)

Twin Lakes

Sixteen miles southwest of Leadville *is the most charming summer resort in Colorado. They* [Twin Lakes] *are situated at the eastern base of the Sawache* [sic] *Range of mountains, at an altitude of 9,333 feet on Twin Lake Creek . . . . The lakes abound in trout. Boats and tackle are provided at the hotels, and those that could not be happy at Twin Lakes, we fear will find the great hereafter an uncomfortable abiding place* (Crofutt, 1881).

During the summer months tourists from all over Colorado filled the hotels and cottages at Twin Lakes. Few miners, however, had either the time or the money for such recreational activities. (Crofutt, 1881)

Belching behemonths

Illustrations of Rocky Mountain scenery, bustling mining towns, stagecoaches, wildlife, politicians, resorts, and trains dominated the pictorial literature in the 1870s. Seldom did artists draw drab smelters. Yet, mining in Colorado depended on these belching behemoths. Trains bearing ore for the Boston and Colorado Reduction Works (above) near Denver ran nearly twenty-four hours a day. In southwestern Colorado, Durango would soon become the smelting center for the mineral-rich San Juan Mountains. (Crofutt, 1881)

GRANT SMELTER. LEADVILLE.

Wonderfully successful smelters

Wonderfully successful, it is through them [the smelters], *more than any one agency, that the City* [Leadville] *owes its present size and importance. The most prominent works are those of the Grand Smelting Company* [above]. By 1880 Grant Smelting *operated seven large stacks and had produced more than $4,000,000 worth of bullion* (Dill, 1881). (South Park railroad booklet)

Smelting Ore in Colorado

One does not find silver and gold in shiny chunks. Rather, an experienced geologist, or crusty old miner with a keen eye, meticulously searches for that illusive vein of ore infused with precious minerals. Promising hunks of ore are retrieved and assayed. If the ore assays "rich," meaning a ton of ore will yield several ounces of silver or gold, the miners begin extracting the ore by whatever means possible. To separate the precious metal from the ore requires smelting. The following sequence of illustrations highlights a few of the smelting processes. The end result is a stack of shiny silver or gold bricks. (All from *Harper's Weekly*, May 30, 1874)

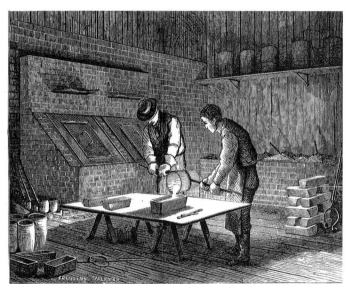

The problem with smelters: *Wholesale murder and suicide*

Smelters also used mercury, cyanide, and arsenic, among other chemcials, to help extract the precious minerals sealed in the ore. Lead was one of the more deadly by-products. Twisting black clouds churning from smelter chimneys spewed various combinations of toxic brews into the atmosphere. Not everyone, even back then, approved.

The only drawback to Leadville [and most other mining towns with smelters] *and our mining interests here, is the poisonous furnace smoke. I believe the association of physicians of this city decided a few weeks ago that the lead smoke of our smelters was not only not deleterious to the health of our people, but that it was really beneficial to health. I presume that was the first time in the history of the world, that a learned body of physicians ever decided that the inhaling of the poisonous fumes and vapors of a lead furnace was beneficial to human health . . . . It is purely a matter of wholesale murder and suicide to allow the smelters to remain in or near Leadville. This question might as well be met at once . . . . Let the doctors successfully controvert what I have said if they can* (The Daily Chronicle, October 11, 1879). (Harper's New Monthly Magazine, February 1880)

Indian policy

By end of the 1870s Colorado's burgeoning population spread over the state like a hungry amoeba. Nothing stood in its way. Not even other humans. *The present Indian policy, which doubtless looks forward to the localizing and settlement of those roving tribes, is intimately connected with the agricultural development of the West . . . . But these roving sons of the Plains know nothing of agriculture, they know nothing of the principles of irrigation, and hence they must be taught, and to do this the locality for each tribe must be fixed, and the experiment tried . . . Unless they are localized and made to enter upon agricultural and pastoral pursuits they must ultimately be exterminated* (Wallihan and Bigney, 1870). (Chicago and Northwestern Railway Company stock certificate)

A legacy of conflict

Most citizens of the United States, including those from Colorado, shared a legacy of conflict with the indigenous peoples of North America. Cultural clashes began in the colonial era (above) and continue today. From the native peoples' perspective, there is no way to sugar-coat this. The *inevitable progress of Euro-American civilization* meant inevitable genocide to many of their tribes and nations. (*Scribner's Monthly,* August 1876)

Phrenology: The study of the conformation of the skull based on a belief that it is indicative of character and mental capacity. (*The American Heritage Dictionary*)

Physiognomy: The art of judging human character from facial features. (*The American Heritage Dictionary*)

Fig. 82.

Fig. 91.

Perceptions of the *American Indian*

*W*hile a great breadth of the base of the brain indicates morbid susceptibilities, yet these, in the Indian, are opposed by a superior height of the skull. Consequently, he is restless, impulsive, excitable, passionate, a vagrant upon the earth . . . . His habits alternate from laziness to heroic effort, from idleness and quiet to the fierce excitement of the chase, from vagabondism to war, sometimes indolent and at other times turbulent, but under all circumstances, irregular and unreliable. In this case, lacteal activity is greater than lymphatic, as his nomadic life indicates. Nevertheless, he manifests a morbid sensibility to epidemic diseases, especially those which engender nutritive disorders and corrupt the blood. Figs. 83 and 84 [opposite page] represent the brain of an American Indian, and that of a European, and show the remarkable difference between their anatomical configuration. Evidently it is a race-distinction . . . . Syphilitic poison, small-pox, and strong drink will annihilate all these tribes sooner than gunpowder (Pierce, 1875). (Pierce, 1875)

Perceptions of an *American*

*W*e desire to offer one more illustration of a marvelous blending of . . . temperament with large mental and emotional faculties. Fig. 91 [above] is a representation of the martyred President, Abraham Lincoln. During an eventful career, his temperament and constitution experienced marked changes, and while always distinguished for strength of purpose and corresponding physical endurance, he was governed by noble, moral faculties, manifesting the deepest sympathy for the down-trodden and oppressed, blending kindness and displaying a genuine compassion, which endeared him to all hearts. He was hopeful, patriotic, magnanimous even, while upholding the majesty of the law and administrating the complicated affairs of government. The balances of his temperament operated with wonderful delicacy, through all the pertubating influences of the rebellion . . . . His life exhibited . . . . a sublime, moral heroism, elements of character which hallow his name, and embalm it in everlasting remembrance (Pierce, 1875). (Pierce, 1875)

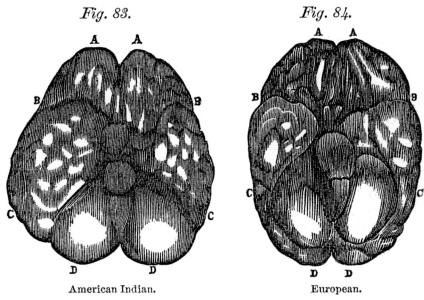

Fig. 83.   *Fig. 84.*

American Indian.   European.

(FROM MORTON'S CRANIA AMERICANA.)

In the American Indian, the anterior lobe, lying between *A A* and *B B*, is small, and in the European it is large, in proportion to the middle, lying between *B B* and *C C.* In the American Indian, the posterior lobe, lying between *C* and *D*, is much smaller than in the European. In the American, the cerebral convolutions on the anterior lobe and upper surface of the brain, are smaller than the European. If the anterior lobe manifest the intellectual faculties—the middle lobe, the propensities common to man with the lower animals—and the posterior lobe, the conservative energies, the result seems to be, that the intellect of the native American will be comparatively feeble—the European, strong; the animal propensities of the Indian will be great—in the European, more moderate; while reproduction, vital energy and conservation of the species of the Indian is not as great as with the European. The relative proportions of the different parts of the brain, differ very materially.

American Indian and European brain

This peculiar [physiognomical and phrenological] *organization* [of the American Indian] *cannot blend in healthful harmony with that of the European, and furthermore, it shows that race-temperaments require separate and careful analytic considerations* (Pierce, 1875). (Pierce, 1875)

Where barbarism and civilization come in contact

Our drawing represents a party of Indians belonging to the Ute tribe, who have come into a border town for the purpose of trading . . . . Indian cunning, supreme in border strategy, is never a match for the sharpened craftiness of the white trader in a bargain . . . . The Indians depicted in our illustration, which is engraved from a sketch of an actual scene witnessed by our artists, appear to have just arrived in town . . . Scenes similar to the one depicted here in our drawing may be witnessed in every frontier town were barbarism and civilization come in contact (Harper's Weekly, July 3, 1875).

Of one Indian Agent a young army bride wrote: And of all unkempt, unshorn, disagreeable-looking personages who had ever stepped into our quarters, this was the worst . . . Heaven save us from a Government which appoints such men as that to watch over and deal with Indians (Summerhayes, 1911). (Harper's Weekly, July 3, 1875)

Disgracefully worthless

After the United States government wrested Indians from their homelands, it frequently "granted" them reservations and annuities in the form of goods. The Utes from the San Juan Mountains in western Colorado were placed on reservations in southern Colorado and Utah Territory. Indian supply trains, like the one shown here, were to bring the Utes *a perpetual yearly annuity of $25,000 — mostly in the form of goods.* The supply trains seldom came. When the trains did arrive, according to the Territorial Governor, the goods proved to be *disgracefully worthless, rotten, and disgusting and might reasonably have been made the ground of revocations of the treaty* (Buys, 1993). (Crofutt, 1881)

An Indian Agency-Distributing Rations

Once a month a crowd of Indians, most of them squaws, assemble at the agency to receive their allotted rations, consisting of flour, coffee, sugar, beef, etc., and return loaded down to their respective homes. The night following is devoted to feasting and revelry, without a thought of the weeks they must starve before another distributing day comes. Proverbially improvident and shiftless, the Indian rarely takes thought for the morrow. While food lasts he will feast; when there is none he will stoically go hungry (Harper's Weekly, November 13, 1875).

Black Elk spoke of this situation: *Once we were happy in our country and we were seldom hungry, for then the two-leggeds and the four-leggeds live together like relatives, and there was plenty for them and for us. But the Wasichus came, and they have made little islands for us and other little islands for the four-leggeds, and always these islands are becoming small, for around them surges the gnawing flood of the Wasichu; and it is dirty with lies and greed* (Black Elk Speaks, 1932). (Harper's Weekly, November 13, 1875)

Form 2.

IMPROVED ORDER OF RED MEN.
HUNTING GROUNDS OF LEADVILLE, COLO.
Wigwam of Navajoe Tribe, No. 9.

..........Sun,.......... ....Moon, G. S. D...........

To the Keeper of Wampum:

Pay to the order of...
.............................*Fa*..................................*F*.......................*In*.

and charge the same to the account of Voucher No.......................

....*Sachem*.

.....*Fa*.....*Ft*.....*In*. ....*Chief of Records*.

RED MEN'S REGALIA, BOOKS & SUPPLIES,
W. J. DINSMORE,
521 WASHINGTON ST., BOSTON, MASS.

Improved Order of Red Men

This fraternity of men attracted members in several Colorado mining towns. No Indians, of course, were allowed. Mining towns did not care for real Indians. For example, on October 11, 1879 — shortly after a *Ute Massacre* in Meeker (see pages 129-131) — Leadville's *The Daily Chronicle* carried a column with the following brief comments:

The Pitkin boom: the Utes must go.

Millions of bullets for savage hearts
but not a cent for annuity.

Go to church to-morrow and pray for
the extermination of the Utes.

It is to be hoped that Butcher
Douglass did not extend his protecting
arm to Father Meeker's family.
Western people too well know what that
protection means, and the reasons which
impelled the brute chief to spare their
lives. [see opposite page]

'The Utes should be hunted like wild
beasts.' What an admirable subject
for a Sunday sermon for one of our
local divines. Who speaks first?
Extermination from a Bible standpoint
would be interesting and would draw a
crowded house.

Butcher Douglass in the German version of *Frank Leslie's Illustrated Newspaper*

The caption reads: *Douglas, First Chief of the White River Ute Indians.* (*Frank Leslie's Illustrated Newspaper* [Germany], November 15, 1879)

Making bullets

I n 1877, women workers assemble cartridges *in one of the buildings of the Union Metallic Cartridge Company, at Bridgeport, Connecticut. This company, and the Winchester Repeating Arms Company, at New Haven, are at present filling large orders . . . . The metallic cartridge shell is of quite recent origin. It was invented by a European, but perfected by American ingenuity and skill (Harper's Weekly,* October 13, 1877). Thousands upon thousands of these metallic cartridges found their way to the West to the "Indian Wars." (Both from *Harper's Weekly,* October 13, 1877)

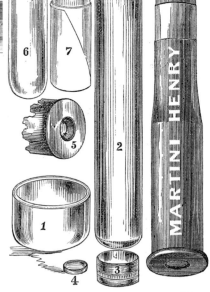

1. Cup. 2. Drawn Shell. 3. Re-enforce. 4. Primer.
5. Base of Shell, showing Cup for Primer. 6. Slug.
7. Patched Bullet. 8. Finished Cartridge.

One of the most thrilling and romantic stories of Indian life

On September 29, 1879, Major Thomas T. Thornburgh's command entered the White River Reservation near Milk Creek, less than twenty miles from the agency, as a show of support for the puritanical and controversial Indian agent, Nathan C. Meeker. By evening, Major Thornburgh and several of his troops were dead. Dead too, seventeen miles away, was Nathan Meeker. The Utes killed the other males at the agency and took all five females of the Meeker and Price families captive. For the next seven days, Thornburgh's men remained pinned down near Milk Creek, caught in the Utes' deadly crossfire.

The narrative of the Ute massacre at the White River Agency, in the northwestern portion of Colorado, the fight with Major Thornburgh's men, and the relief of the beleaguered survivors by a company of colored cavalry is, in a few words, one of the most thrilling and romantic stories of Indian life. For quickness of action, baseness of motive and cruelty of execution, it far surpasses any of those episodes that were so graphically clothed in simple English by Fennimore Cooper (Frank Leslie's Illustrated Newspaper, *November 8, 1879). (*Frank Leslie's Illustrated Newspaper, *November 8, 1879)*

African-American troops boost trapped command

On the fourth day (October 2, 1879) of the siege, Captain Francis Dodge and his African-American troops rode in to assist the trapped command. Reflecting on his experience with these African-American troops, a soldier said: *We took those darkies in right along with us in the pits. We let'em sleep with us, and they took their knives and cut off slips of bacon from the same sides as we did.* Early newspaper story had Thornburgh's troops greeting these soldiers *as though they were the purest of caucasians.* Commenting on the value of the blacks, an officer in the battle volunteered that they were *the whitest blackmen I ever saw* (Buys, 1986). (*Harper's Weekly,* November 1, 1879)

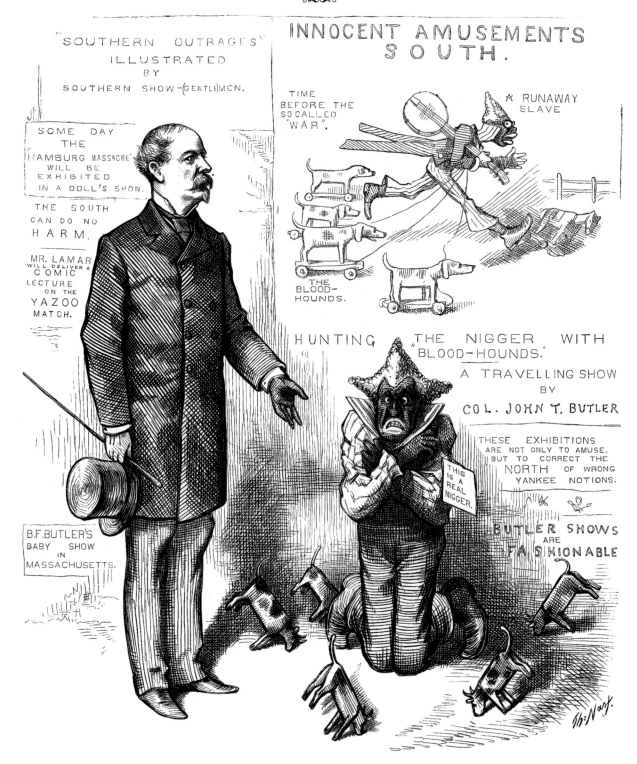

On the front page

The image on the previous page, featuring the heroic exploits of the African-American troops, was printed in an issue that carried the cover shown above. (*Harper's Weekly*, November 1, 1879)

Rescue of the besieged command

Finally, at least from the soldiers' perspective, a relief force arrived under the command of General Wesley Merritt. Dawn had barely broken on the morning of October 5, 1879, when, bugles blaring, about 200 cavalrymen charged into the entrenchments to be welcomed by the deliriously happy troops. The Utes, who had seen them coming, showed a white flag and soon dispersed into the colorful mosaic of the Colorado mountains. The battle of Milk Creek was over (Buys, 1986). (*Frank Leslie's Illustrated Newspaper*, November 8, 1879)

Four of the female captives

The relief troops advanced to the White River Agency to find all the men dead and the women missing. According to one account, Nathan Meeker had a log chain cinched around his neck and a barrel stave driven through his throat. The Utes said he talked to much (Buys, 1986). Almost three weeks later the relief column finally secured the release of all five females. The possibility of *indignities visited upon Miss Meeker* [above] *and Mrs. Price* [above] remained a point of contention in the press. (*Frank Leslie's Illustrated Newspaper,* November 22, 1879)

Chief Ouray

Intelligent, dignified, and gracious, Chief Ouray held off the white man's onslaught as long as he could. It was said of the sophisticated and multilingual Ouray: *Never in all his dealings with the whites did he show himself other than their friend.* Some say he saved the Utes from complete annihilation. After he died in 1889 the demise of the once great Ute nation followed quickly. Today the Utes occupy reservations in southern Colorado and northeastern Utah. (Bank of Ouray check)

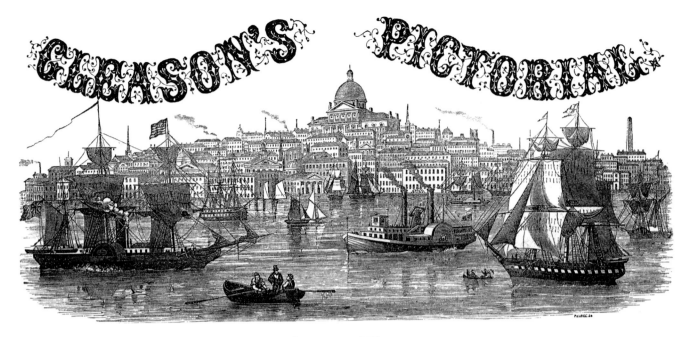

Chapter Three
The Price of Progress
(1880s - 1890s)

Colorado may never see another two decades like those that closed the nineteenth century. In this chapter more than one hundred illustrations highlight Colorado's incredible transition from a booming frontier state to one beset by financial crises and deadly labor strife. Yet one thing has remained the same — the people keep coming. As witnessed within these pages, some of the best visual symbols we have from this era are drawn images.

In the 1880s mining still sustained Colorado. By 1885, however, over half a million cattle and three-quarters of a million sheep contributed substantially to the state's economy. From this booming cattle industry came the enduring image of the "cowboy," a favorite subject of nineteenth-century illustrators and twentieth-century Hollywood. Meanwhile, tourists and "sportsmen"

flocked to Colorado's scenic and game-rich environs. By 1886, hard working farmers had already cultivated more than 4,000,000 acres of land on the east and west slopes of Colorado.

In the latter decades of the nineteenth century, disease and starvation — caused mainly by the slaughter of the great buffalo herds — decimated the Indian population. Those who survived were unceremoniously forced onto reservations in Colorado and Utah. Then the United States Department of Interior shipped thousands of Indian children to all-Indian trade schools back East. There they learned the white man's language, customs, and trades so that they could be gainfully employed in the American workplace. Americans of Chinese and African descent fared better than the Indians but not much. As the following illustrations show, Chinese Americans and African Americans also felt the sharp social and economic sting of a society dominated by Anglo-American males. When more polygynous Mormons began moving into Colorado, they, too, were judged to be a threat to the "American way of life." Lastly, long downtrodden women began to fight for what they felt was right. Intrepid female crusaders demanded that alcohol be banned and that national suffrage be passed. Neither happened. Recently, however, popular books have focused on women who worked, traveled, and prospered on the Colorado frontier. Many welcome this "revisionist" literature as a counterbalance to the disproportionate number of books that have focused solely on "ladies of the evening."

By 1890 the population of Colorado exceeded 400,000 — ten times the pre-1870 number. Most of the inhabitants arrived in Denver by rail from the East and Midwest. The burgeoning capital city also accounted for most of the state's premier public buildings, hospitals, churches, and institutions of higher learning. No longer a frontier town, Denver's newspapers carried illustrated advertisements touting the most recent goods and fashions for increasingly sophisticated socialites.

Although some people may disagree, the heart and soul of Colorado lay well beyond the confines of urban Denver — in the pristine Rocky Mountains. Railroad companies, whose main business was the mining business, clearly understood this over a century ago. They attracted thousands of customers with striking images and glowing descriptions of snowcapped mountain ranges, healthful mineral springs, otherworldly rock formations, dense forests teeming with game, streams rolling with trout, and precipitous canyons churning with rushing blue waters.

Then came the bad times. In July 1893, the United States government chose to place its monetary faith in gold, not silver. It repealed the Sherman Silver Purchase Act that had kept the price of silver inordinately high. Overnight the price of silver dropped drastically. Colorado's economy collapsed. Smelters and most silver mines shut down, banks closed, jobs were lost, and real estate values tumbled. The danger of widespread hunger prompted the organization of relief committees in mining camps. Bread lines were established in Denver for the destitute. Fortunately, new mining towns — with gold as their base — had burst onto the scene in the early 1890s. The soaring population of Colorado's new savior, Cripple Creek, soon ranked second in the state. Meanwhile, in the San Juan Mountains of southwestern Colorado, renewed interest in gold mining and new gold discoveries near Creede, Ouray, Silverton, and Telluride helped sustain the state's mining industry.

More trouble followed. For years miners in Colorado had labored under slave-like conditions with abysmal pay (perhaps $3.00 a day). Indeed, seven days a week miners faced the specter of injury and death from unsafe and unhealthy working conditions. From their labors, only a few owners profited handsomely. After the silver crisis, miners' wages dropped even further. Finally, the miners had had enough. Violent labor strife spread throughout Colorado. Marshall Law became the norm in many mining towns. Ultimately, the beleaguered miners had neither enough money nor clout to sustain the strikes. They went back to work under the same conditions and for the same miserable pay.

Despite Colorado's economic woes and labor disputes, the centennial state still stood tall at the end of the nineteenth century. Attracted by its unsurpassed beauty and healthful climate, people just kept coming. A more diversified economy emerged. Yet one turn-of-the-century illustrator lamented that it was "almost a pity" that even outlying Glenwood Springs was becoming so famous. Too many people now crowded the pool.

The real star of my Westerns has always been the land

Early movie producer John Ford made this observation after filming **Stagecoach** which starred Marion Morrison under the name of John Wayne. The real attraction of Colorado has also always been the land. Here frontier artist Thomas Moran sketched imposing Longs Peak in the early 1880s. (Crofutt, 1881)

Fantastic scenery of some disordered dream

*O*pposite Currecanti Needle and cañon stand some very remarkable rocks, underneath the greatest of which the train passes . . . . And so, past wonder after wonder, Pelion upon Ossa, buried a huge rocky prison, yet always in the full sunlight, you suddenly swing around a sharp corner, leaving the Gunnison to go on through ten miles more of cañon, and crashing noisily through the zig-zag cañon of the Cimmaron, which is so very narrow and dark it deserves no better name than crevice, quickly emerges into daylight . . . . (Ingersoll, 1885). (Ingersoll, 1885)

The Cow-Boys of Colorado — part of the landscape

The 'cow-boys' of the Rocky Mountain region are a race or a class peculiar to that country. They have some resemblance to the corresponding class on the southern side of the Rio Grande, but are of a milder and more original type. In the Great herding districts, where cattle are fattened in great part upon the public domain, and roam, winter and summer, over vast areas without fences, without roads, and with only scattered and irregular places for water and shelter, the herdsmen play an important industrial role. It is their business to keep the cattle as nearly together as possible, to guide them to the springs and wooded hollows, to separate them when they get mixed up with those of other droves, to brand them at the proper seasons, and to drive them to the nearest market at others (Harper's Weekly, October 6, 1883). (Harper's Weekly, October 6, 1883)

A Cowboy

There are both good and bad cowboys . . . but the class as a whole has been grossly maligned. One reason for this is that the cowboy is a favorite dime-novel hero; another is that he is not himself averse to humoring the exaggerated notions of 'tenderfoot' visitors from the East, and passing himself off as a desperado — what is called in the frontier vernacular 'a cutter and a shooter from away back.' In reality, as we have said, he is an honest, industrious, brave, whole-souled fellow, and probably has a little claim or farm of his own. Many of the cowboys are from Eastern cities. There are rich men's sons and college graduates among them. A surprisingly large number of them are well-read and intelligent, while not a few can solve a mathematical problem or parse a Latin sentence with as much ease as they can throw a steer or punch a brand (Frank Leslie's Illustrated Newspaper, April 9, 1887). (Frank Leslie's Illustrated Newspaper, April 9, 1887)

Pitching Broncos and Branding a Steer

The cowboy is necessarily a hard worker, and his earnings do not average over thirty or forty dollars a month, with his 'finding,' during the five or six months of the year which give him employment at his regular occupations (Frank Leslie's Illustrated Newspaper, April 9, 1887). (Both from Frank Leslie's Illustrated Newspaper, April 9, 1887)

A liberal flask of whiskey

*The outfit of the cow-boy is a horse, usually one of the 'ponies' of the region — swift, tough, ugly in look and temper, but capable of good service when once trained; a Mexican or 'army' saddle, such as are shipped in great quantities from New York; a blanket, or with the best herdsmen, a pair, one being of rubber; one or more pistols, sometimes a rifle; and, with great uniformity, a liberal flask of whiskey (*Harper's Weekly, *October 6, 1883). (*Frank Leslie's Illustrated Newspaper, *April 9, 1887)*

The finest types of physical manhood in the world

The round-up keeps the men on the prairie for days and weeks together. They camp, eat and sleep under the open sky, watching their herds night and day, chasing stragglers heading off stampedes, and experiencing all those hardships and adventures which develop some of the finest types of physical manhood in the world (Frank Leslie's Illustrated Newspaper, April 9, 1887). (Frank Leslie's Illustrated Newspaper, April 9, 1887)

The Cow-Boys of Colorado — Life in a Dug-Out

Life in these unique habitations is very cozy and comfortable. Their construction renders them an equally good defense against the severity of winter storms and the attacks of hostile Indians. Cellar-like, as the name implies, and with substantial bullet-proof roof, sometimes covered with earth, with a roaring fire on the hearth, they are as secure as a fortress . . . . In these comfortable quarters the cow-boys pass the time in various ways-some playing cards, others mumble-the-peg, others in reading. There is a good deal of monotony in this sort of existence, but the boys find abundant compensation in the wild excitements of their out-door life (Harper's Weekly, November 18, 1882). (Harper's Weekly, November 18, 1882)

Sheep Raid in Colorado

The owners of cattle herds in the great Southwest are sworn enemies of the sheep-raisers, on the ground, real or fanciful, that sheep injure the grazing lands. Some time such scenes as the one represented in our engraving [above] . . . were of frequent occurrence in parts of Colorado. A party of cattle-owners, disguised and closely muffled, have surprised a sheep-raiser just before sunrise. While two keep him and his assistant cowed by the exhibition of six-shooters, the others make sad havoc among the defenseless sheep, killing and maiming them with revolvers and clubs. These outrages have been checked by the sheep-raisers forming combinations of their own defense, and keeping armed watch over their flocks (Harper's Weekly, October 13, 1877). (Harper's Weekly, October 13, 1877)

RESULT OF IRRIGATION.

MAKING A START.

"LIFTING WHEELS ON THE GUNNISON."

THE BAD LANDS.

Domesticating the land

In some counties of the State irrigating canals, carrying large streams of water, taken out of the mountain rivers, near the mountains, have been built, extending for fifty miles or more over the plains, from which innumerable small ditches conduct water over the fields of the farmers, thus insuring good crops, as irrigation is necessary on nearly all tillable land in the State; yet there are a few patches along the river bottoms and about springs where crops can be raised without irrigation, but they are liable to be destroyed at any time by overflow or too much water (Crofutt, 1881). (Harper's Weekly, November 20, 1886)

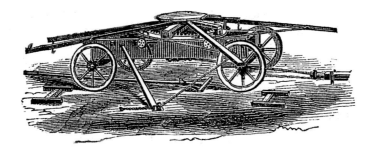

Farm machinery for Colorado crops

Wheat yields from 30 to 50 bushels to the acre and other small grains do well. Corn, except in Boulder and Larimer counties and vicinity, is not a success as compared with some eastern states. Vegetables of all kinds do remarkably well in all parts of the State where the land is supplied with water. In the southwestern portion of the State, in La Plata and Conejos counties, we have seen vegetables in the fields and markets unsurpassed in abundance, flavor and size by any portion of the older States (Crofutt, 1881). (*The Denver Daily Tribune,* November 15, 1876)

The Hunter's Paradise

The hills . . . are covered with dense forests of pine, in which game, such as bear, elk, and deer, are abundant (Wallihan and Bigney, 1870).

   For game, it [Colorado] has no equal in the world. Bison, wild cattle, deer, elk, antelope, bear, mountain sheep, grouse and quail abound, together with grizzlies and mountain lions . . . (Crofutt, 1881). (Crofutt, 1881)

The Big-Horn

Another prized game animal, big-horn sheep, never grew horns like these — even in Colorado. (*Golden Days for Boys and Girls,* April 8, 1893)

Rabbit meat

Though not a popular food, rabbit meat still provided many a meal for early homesteaders and miners. (Crofutt, 1881)

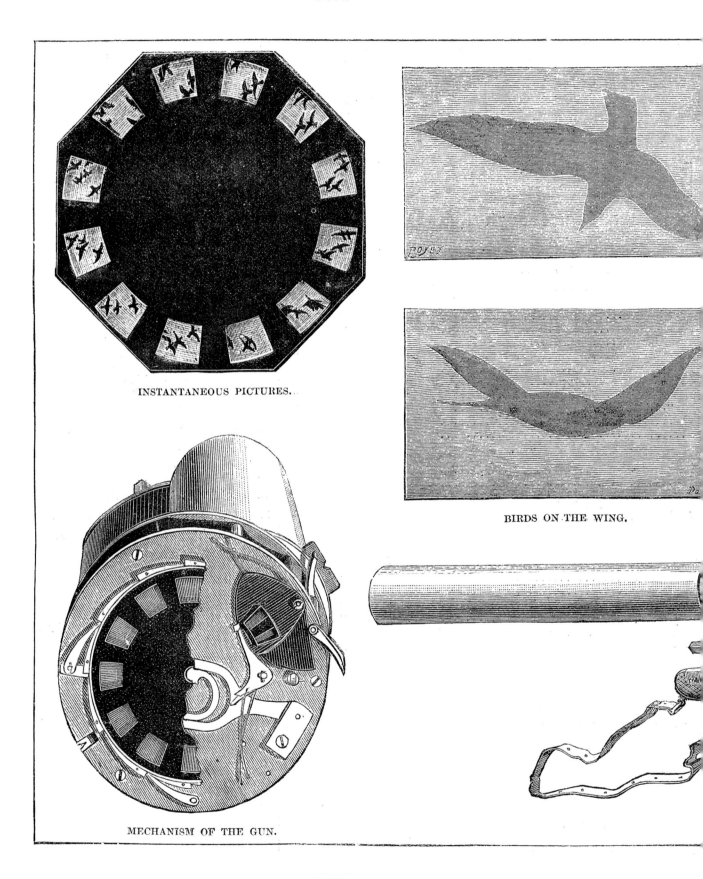

INSTANTANEOUS PICTURES.

BIRDS ON THE WING.

MECHANISM OF THE GUN.

Not everyone came to kill

This implement [photographic gun] *is neither more nor less than a very large revolver, with a stock to put to the shoulder. The barrel is a telescope; that is to say, it contains the lenses of a camera. There are twelve apertures, which take the place of the chambers. The photographer puts in a sensitized plate behind these apertures, and performing an operation analogous to cocking the weapon, he is ready for the field. On seeing a flying bird, he takes aim, and pulls the trigger; the chamber revolves once, and in one second he obtains twelve little pictures of the bird in various positions* (Harper's Weekly, May 27, 1882). (Harper's Weekly, May 27, 1882)

TAKING AIM.

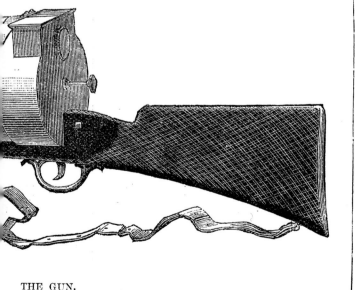

THE GUN.

No photographic guns for buffalo: "A War of Extermination"

For centuries an estimated sixty million buffalo thrived within the geographic boundaries of present-day United States. Then came the white man; and the slaughter began. By the early 1870s professional hunters and "Eastern and European Sportsmen" killed over 1,000,000 buffalo annually. By 1887 this extraordinary animal could no longer be found in Colorado, nor could most of the Plains Indians who depended on them for food, clothing, and shelter.

On August 2, 1884, *Harper's Weekly* carried this illustration and an article entitled "A War of Extermination": *At the time of the discovery of this country its entire temperate zone, from Central America to the arctic regions, and from ocean to ocean, was a buffalo range. White men saw and killed them within thirty miles of the site now occupied by the city of Charleston, South Carolina; in Virginia and Pennsylvania they were traced to the sea-board; and though no evidence remained to show that they ever ranged east of the Hudson or Lake Champlain, there was also none to prove the contrary. Like the fowls of the air, they migrated from North to South, and back again with the changing seasons, and their trails, invariably seeking the easiest grades and safest crossing-places of rivers, were the pioneers of wagon roads and railways. Fifty years ago the magnificent beasts inhabited the vast territory between the Mississippi River and the Rocky Mountains in such countless numbers that they were estimated by millions, and it was supposed that the supply of buffalo meat and robes in this country were absolutely inexhaustible. It was only in 1870 that a writer in HARPER'S MONTHLY MAGAZINE laughed at the fears of the Indians that the buffalo would soon be exterminated, and declared such fears to be groundless. To-day, less than fifteen years from that date, the buffalo has practically disappeared from this country, and a few small herds, one on the Pecos River in Texas, and two or three in the extreme North, are all that remain of the millions a decade ago. Even these are surrounded by an army of butchers, who slaughter them as ruthlessly as though they were vermin and their speedy destruction was imperatively demanded . . . . The United States has even encouraged their extermination.*

As for the indigenous human populations . . .

It is an established fact that many centuries ago portions of this State were inhabited by a race of people of whom we have no authentic history, but they are generally supposed to be descendants of the Astec [sic] and Toltec races, (a few of which are still to be found in old Mexico). Without doubt these ancient people were exterminated or driven out of the country by the tribes of Indians found occupying it when discovered by the whites. Here then is an argument to refute the claim that 'this is the Indian's country.' The Aztecs and Toltecs owned the country. The Indians succeeded them. The whites succeeded the Indians. Will the time come when the present succession will be succeeded by a stronger? Will the present white race, in turn, be driven out and exterminated? — Quin Sabe (Crofutt, 1881).

The illustration on the opposite page is a fanciful rendition of impossibly perched "Aztec and Toltec cliff dwellings" in western Colorado. (Crofutt, 1881)

◆ *A More Appreciative Race* ◆

The western . . . slope of Colorado . . . abounds in finely watered, fertile and undulating prairies, and when made accessible to the arts of civilization will be found to offer great inducements to all classes of settlers. The southern half of this slope is embraced in the consolidated reservation of the Ute tribe of Indians, and is, therefore, ineligible for occupation by whites; but these savage tribes are all waning, and must finally become extinct, leaving their rich possessions to be occupied and developed by a more appreciative race (Wallihan and Bigney, 1870).

Wards of the United States Government

*W*here once roamed his 'pony herd,' in thousands, now can be counted the dwellings of his successors in equal numbers; where once the Indian's beef (buffalo) ranged in untold millions, now range the white man's beef. The buffalo has gone . . . (Crofutt, 1881). In place of the Indians' land and the buffalo came annual payments (above), often in the form of cheap trade goods and rotten food. By the early 1880s, Native Americans were fast becoming the wards of the United States government. (*Ballou's Pictorial Drawing-Room Companion* [early 1880s, specific date unknown])

Sneaking, wily, treacherous, and cruel

The United States military, often with the help of Indian guides, doggedly pursued recalcitrant Indians who refused to accept handouts, let alone stay on their "assigned" reservations.

In the above sketch, *the young lieutenant, fresh from his studies on the banks of the Hudson, who finds himself for the first time in command of a scouting party in the Indian country, is placed in a most trying situation. Brave, gallant, and thoroughly versed in the theory of what is called 'civilized war,' he now confronts an enemy whose way of fighting is entirely new to him — sneaking, wily, treacherous, and cruel. But with trusty and experienced men at his side, he quickly learns the duties of his new position, and in a few months becomes a skillful frontier soldier* (Harper's Weekly, November 18, 1882). (*Harper's Weekly*, November 18, 1882)

The Ute Scare in Colorado

The first collision in the present trouble between the whites and the Utes under Colorado took place on Tuesday, August 9th [1887], *at Beaver Creek, Col. On that occasion Colorow and eighty of his warriors were surprised while in camp* [a hunting camp outside the reservation] *by the sheriff's posse sent against them. The skirmish which followed resulted in the wounding of four of the Indians and the flight of the whole band. The situation at that time was regarded as serious, and reports from the scene of the disturbance during the past two weeks have warranted the fear of an alarming Indian outbreak . . . . The effect which this news had upon these comparatively helpless people* [shown left] *may be easily imagined. Aid from the State troops stationed in Denver could not be expected for several days, and, while the women and children huddled together in the two hotels of the place* [Meeker], *the one hundred and fifty men present armed themselves and prepared to defend the town against assault . . . . Later reports from Meeker state that the Indians have withdrawn to a considerable distance from the town, and the excitement and terror of the inhabitants have in a measure subsided . . . . The general belief is that the 'scare' amongst the white settlers has been disproportionate to the amount of the real danger (Frank Leslie's Illustrated Newspaper, November 3, 1887). (Frank Leslie's Illustrated Newspaper, November 3, 1887)*

In Pursuit of Colorow

A body of 350 men, including 236 State troops, are looking for Colorow and his band, who in some manner knows everything that is going on, and has established himself in a secure place in the mountains. Colorow has avoided the troops and scouts thus far, but it is believed that a meeting will occur, and that there will be fighting (Frank Leslie's Illustrated Newspaper, September 3, 1887). (Harper's Weekly, September 3, 1887)

A GOOD LESSON FOR BAD INDIANS.
"How did you like your reception by the Mexicans with open·arms?"

A Good Lesson for Bad Indians

In the early 1880s a few "renegade Indian bands" sought refuge in northern Mexico. Their hostile reception is the theme of the political cartoon shown above. (*Harper's Weekly,* May 27, 1882)

"OVER THE RANGE."

Portrayals in train propaganda

By the late 1880s railroad tourist books frequently featured (see this and the opposite page) idealized images of Indians as inducements for potential customers. In other words: "Ride the trains, see the noble savages." The Colorado Midland Railway incorporated an image of an Indian warrior into its logo. (Wood, 1889)

A Ute Council Fire

Soon such fires would be extinguished throughout the West. (Wood, 1889)

Cartoon stereotypes

Cartoonists throughout the United States often skewered politicians by draping them with the accoutrements of an Indian chief. Ironically, the "Society of Tammany" (notice "Tammany" on the politician's breastplate) took its name from an early Delaware Indian chief known for his wisdom. (*Harper's Weekly*, October 6, 1883)

Trade schools for Indians

In the mid-1880s, under the watchful eye of the United States Secretary of Interior Henry M. Teller of Colorado, thousands of Indian children entered boarding schools. There they were trained in contemporary trades. Teller felt Indian education should no longer be left to "corrupt, broken-down missionaries sent to the reservations." Many people objected to Teller's "unenlightened and liberal policy" toward Indian education. Indians objected because their children were taken from them, transported hundreds of miles away, forced to speak English, and, among other things, dressed in white man's clothes.

On May 27, 1882, *Harper's Weekly* wrote: *They came to the school from the prairies and the mountains, dressed in blankets and moccasins, with uncut and unkempt hair, as wild as young coyotes. They have already learned to sing like nightingales and work like beavers. It is remarkable that these young children of the forest are perfectly amenable to discipline, and never break a rule. The boys learn how to make boots and shoes, build houses, shoe horses, and how to perform the various operations of agriculture. The girls learn to sew, darn, wash, cook, churn, iron, wash dishes, and keep their rooms in order. Both sexes learn their lessons promptly, and retain what they learn tenaciously. The common school games and amusements, playing ball, running races, and the like, are indulged by the boys, while the little girls play with their dolls. They attend religious meetings and lectures, and sing and pray. The singing, indeed, is of remarkable excellence.* (*Harper's Weekly*, May 27, 1882)

HOUSEKEEPING.

CARPENTERS AT WORK

NEW RECRUITS —SPOKANE INDIANS

...AKING.

A SCHOOL SCENE.

'Every Dog' (No Distinction of Color) 'Has His Day'

Subtitled, *Red Gentleman to Yellow Gentleman, 'Pale face 'fraid you crowd him out, as he did me,'* this *Harper's Weekly* cover illustration gives one a sense of the prevailing attitudes toward ethnic minorities in the latter part of the nineteenth century. More specifically, the above image portends the Chinese Exclusion Act of 1882. Thousands of Chinese, fleeing the bloody Peking rebellion in their homeland, had provided cheap and efficient labor for the California gold fields and the construction of the transcontinental railroad.

The majority of Americans (many of them recent immigrants from Europe) felt this massive influx of "cheap Chinese labor" constituted unfair competition for jobs. Consequently, the United States Federal Government passed the Chinese Exclusion Act that restricted the immigration of Chinese into America and required every person of "Chinese origin," even those who had been born in America, to register with the government. The Act also denied Chinese the right to vote. (*Harper's Weekly*, February 8, 1879)

'Oh, you jes' say same's if 'twas yous own, Miss Katie'

Stereotypical treatment of African Americans permeated the popular magazines, journals, and newspapers during the 1880s. (*Harper's Weekly,* February 16, 1884)

Ethnocentric ads

Shown here are illustrated ads for the popular Pearl Baking Powder and well-known Cuticura Remedies. (*The Tribune,* Denver, Colorado, November 23, 1880) (*Frank Leslie's Illustrated Newspaper,* April 9, 1887)

'Proclaim Liberty Throughout all the Land Unto All the Inhabitants Thereof'

Subtitled, '*Listening to the Sound of Liberty and Rejoicing That There is No More Slavery,*' this egualitarian caption is belied by the often subtle yet racially demeaning statements and ads carried by the popular magazine. (*Harper's Weekly,* January 24, 1880)

A Typical Mexican

In 1889 a railroad guidebook for Colorado read: *The traveler will notice that the names of stations have assumed a Spanish form, and should he happen to address any of the swarthy men that chance to be lounging around the stations, he would very likely to receive a reply in the language of Hispania. The Spanish spoken is not Castilian by any means, but is about as near it as 'Pidgin English' is to genuine Chinese, being a mixture of English, Spanish, and Indian dialects (Wood, 1889).* (Wood, 1889)

Utah's Best Crop

In 1881 *Crofutt's Grip-Sack Guide of Colorado* featured this collage-like drawing entitled, *Utah's Best Crop,* on the inside of the back cover. Contemporary newspapers and magazines occasionally portrayed Mormons — and especially their practice of polygyny — as more threatening to the "American way of life" than Indians, African Americans, Chinese Americans, and Mexican Americans combined. Mormons finally forbade polygyny in 1896.

F. T. Stuart, Boston

Attitudes toward women

It took forty-four years after Colorado became a state in 1876 before women could even vote in an election. Indeed, based on the proportion of modern books that feature mining towns' "fallen doves," one might conclude that prostitutes constituted the majority of the female gender in Colorado. Not so. Although considered bad luck in mines, women worked in several professions. For example, in the early 1880s numerous female-owned businesses and four female doctors were listed in the *Leadville City Directory.*

On a national level, Phebe A. Hanaford (above) compiled a book in the early 1880s entitled: *Daughters of America; or Women of the Century.* In it she highlighted numerous women *whose lives were full of usefulness, and therefore worthy of renown and imitation* (Hanaford, 1882). (Hanaford, 1882)

Lady-Physicians

The caption on this illustration read: *Who is this interesting invalid? It is young Reginald De Braces, who has succeeded in Catching a Bad Cold, in order that he might Send for that rising Practitioner, Dr. ARABELLA BOLUS!* (*Harper's Weekly*, January 27, 1866)

First President Woman's National Christian Temperance Union

Although stern women like Mrs. Annie Wittenmeyer (above) had little success in closing down drinking establishments in Colorado, let alone throughout the United States, it did not dampen their fervor. In 1882 a temperance crusader wrote: *The great solemnity pervading the ranks of the crusaders, over against the dark, damp underground retreat, redolent with the fumes of whiskey and beer, made doubly hideous by the jeers and shrieks of those who had rallied around the proprietors, was, to one who had never before entered such a place, the very embodiment of all that was evil. Immediately the full import of the surroundings seized upon my soul; and the fear that this might be the last opportunity impelled me to step upon a chair, and attempt to address them* (Hanaford, 1882). (Hanaford, 1882)

The Grace Darling of America

Some of the Irish-American miners who flocked to Colorado probably took with them the image of Ida Lewis (above). When her parents moved to the Lime Rock Lighthouse off the coast of Massachusetts, *her father becoming paralytic, she was obliged to use the oars, and bring all the supplies to the lighthouse, and row her brothers and sister to and from school. Hence she became an expert rower, and was as fearless on the ocean as others on the land. In the fall of 1858 she first gratified her philanthropic nature, and won a place among the brave, by rescuing four young men from drowning, when their pleasure-boat had been upset through recklessness. She was then but sixteen. Eight years after, when Ida had barely reached the age of Grace Darling, she rescued a drowning soldier from the neighboring fort. In 1867 she rescued three Irishmen who were out in a boat after a sheep which was drifting out to sea. Their skill and courage failed them, and amid the white-capped billows they were powerless to reach the shore; and having taken the men off their sinking boat, and safely landed them, she returned, and rescued also the sheep* (Hanaford, 1882). (Hanaford, 1882)

No place for drones

In 1870 Colorado Territory boasted a population of 39,868. By 1880, Colorado's state population had soared to 155,292. Several "modern" railroads contributed to the growth, although not everyone was welcome: *Coloradoans, as a class, are working people, always busy. It is no place for drones. There is always work of some kind for all those who honestly seek it. Make a name for honesty, sobriety and reliability, and you can soon attain any position and salary that your abilities will warrant. If you are not such a person, stay away from Colorado, and let your friends, if you have any, support you in idleness* (Crofutt, 1881). (Chicago Northwestern Railway Company Stock Certificate: Author's collection)

Superb palaces

These cars, for elegance, finish, convenience, cleanliness and comfort, are without a peer in any land. Think of enjoying one of these superb palaces and partaking of a meal composed of all the substantial, game and delicacies of the season, while running over the smoothest of track in America, and that at the rate of from thirty to forty miles an hour (Crofutt, 1881). No fewer than six railroads ferried thousands of passengers and mountains of freight to Denver and beyond during the 1880s and 1890s. (Crofutt, 1881)

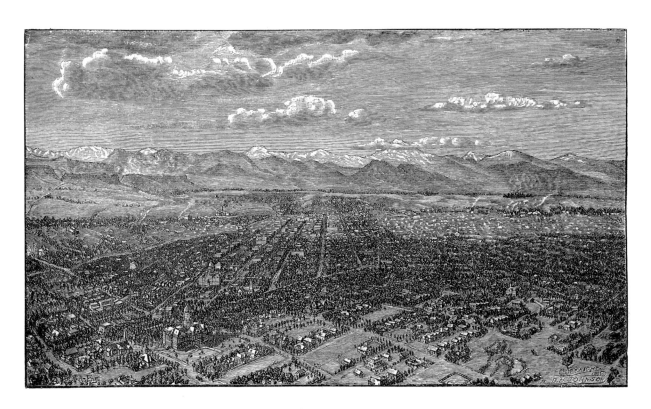

Unsurpassed beauty — a view of Denver from the east

The view of the Rocky Mountains, which the traveler gains on approaching Denver from the east is one of unsurpassed beauty, and that this statement may not rest on the dictum of this book [Over the Range to the Golden Gate, 1889], *let us take the testimony of the greatest traveler, and the most graceful descriptive writer America has yet produced. Bayard Taylor says: ' know no external picture of the Alps that can be placed beside it. If you take away the valley of the Rhine, and unite the Alps of Savoy with the Bernese Overland, you might obtain a tolerable idea of this view of the Rocky Mountains.'* (Wood, 1889)

One falls in love at once with Paris, Denver, or San Francisco

Fourteenth Street in Denver is shown above. Of Denver one writer pined: *There are only a few cities in the world that please at first sight. Denver is one of this favored few. The liking one gets for Boston, Philadelphia or London is an acquired taste, but one falls in love at once with Paris, Denver or San Francisco* (Wood, 1889). (Wood, 1889)

GARSON'S. GARSON'S. GARSON'S. GA

Sartorial splendor

Garson's *One-Price Clothing House* advertised their wares in *The Tribune* (Denver, October 17, 1880). Located at 237 and 239 Fifteenth on the corner of Holladay, it claimed the *Largest Stock in the City!*

Two typical bodices (right) for women appeared in *Frank Leslie's Illustrated Weekly,* March 1, 1894. Women's clothing stores in Denver made certain to carry the latest fashions from the East.

SON'S. GARSON'S. GARSON'S.

Beer, guns, and groceries

Illustrated ads appeared in newspapers, business directories, magazines, tourist guides, and on daily business receipts. During the late nineteenth century, Anheuser-Busch Brewing Association (top), Denver gunsmith John P. Lower (left), Denver Brewing Company (bottom), and the Cornforth and Company food store (right) in Denver all used illustrated ads. (Clockwise: Carl Nollenberger liquor dealer receipt, 1899; Crofutt, 1881; Wood, 1889; and Crofutt 1881)

More illustrated ads — before the Food and Drug Administration

Sozodont: This popular dentifrice is now a recognized essential of every toilet table. It is totally innoxious, CONTAINING NO ACID, and for preserving and CLEANSING THE TEETH, and retaining the normal condition of the gums, it has no rival (*Harper's Weekly*, April 9, 1892).

Madame Rowley's Toilet Mask: Complexion blemishes may be hidden imperfectly by cosmetics and powders, but can only be removed permanently by the Toilet Mask. By its use every kind of spots, impurities, roughness, etc., vanish from the skin, leaving it soft, clear, brilliant and beautiful (*Frank Leslie's Illustrated Newspaper*, April 9, 1887).

Duffy's Pure Malt Whisky

Testimonials — Chas. Blackford: My wife had been sick with malarial fever, and your Duffy's Pure Malt Whisky cured her.

— H. C. Darlington: I tried your Duffy's Pure Malt Whisky and Duffy's Formula. I have been troubled ten years with the ague. We will use nothing else hereafter for medicial [sic] *use.*

— Mr. Mittnacht writes: That his case of dyspepsia he considered hopeless. Duffy's Pure Malt Whiskey [sic] *cured him in a short time* (The National Republican Senatorial Edition, 1886).

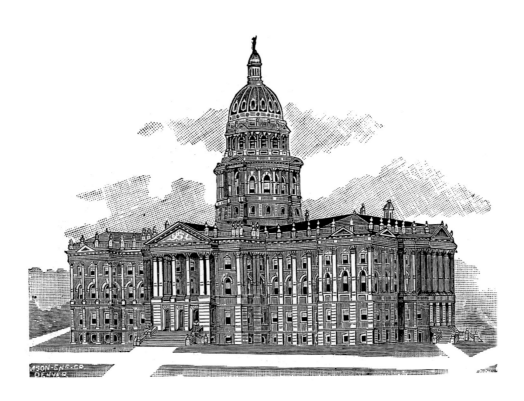

Colorado's State Capitol Building, Denver

The town [Denver] *is lighted by gas and electricity, has paid fire and police departments, and obtains its water from mountain sources by means of Holly works, and from over 300 artesian wells varying in depth from 350 to 1,600 feet. The public buildings, exclusive of churches and schools, cost $4,000,000. The real estate belonging to the city is worth $2,000,000, the bonded debt is only $400,000 and the assessed valuation of Denver is $37,500,000. The commerce of Denver is now annually not less than one hundred millions of dollars.*

One feels a sense of exhilaration in the atmosphere of Denver (Wood, 1889). (Wood, 1889)

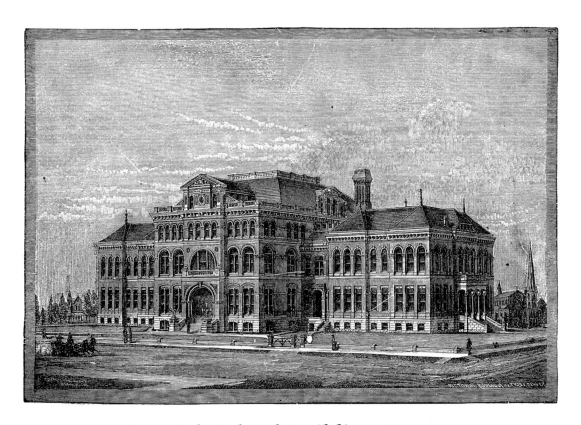

The High School Building, Denver

In 1867, Owen J. Goldrick organized Denver's first public school. In 1875, seventeen-year-old Jessie Forshee received the first high school diploma awarded in the state of Colorado from the all-girls St. Mary's Academy.

Shown above is Denver's imposing high school building in 1889. (Wood, 1889)

The Pitiful Fate of Our Overworked School Children

The superintendents and teachers of our public schools should look to the digestive power of a child's brain instead of endeavoring to gorge it with a quantity of food that must eventually weaken and perhaps destroy it altogether. Away with infant prodigies! Can any picture be more harrowing than that of childhood overworked? The listless attitude where all should be nervous vitality; the sunken eyes, where two twinkling stars should be shining; the pallid cheek, where the red roses of health should be blooming; the watery smile, where condensed sunlight should be glittering! That the course of school studies for the upper classes of our public schools is worse than a crime — a blunder — is an established fact (Frank Leslie's Illustrated Newspaper, November 11, 1882). (Frank Leslie's Illustrated Newspaper, November 11, 1882)

The Building of the National Mining and Industrial Exposition, Denver, Colorado (1882)

The entire world has been invited to participate in the Exposition; an act of Congress has been passed exempting from import duty goods designed for the Exposition, and many foreign manufacturers have signified their intention to display their wares . . . . The main building of the Exposition, which is now being constructed, resembles in many respects the new National Museum Building at Washington, D.C. The materials used in its construction are stone, brick, iron, and glass, and it is intended as a permanent repository of ores and geological specimens, as well as every variety of improved mining machinery . . . . The floor space in the main building will be more than 150,000 square feet, while three or four times that amount of space will be offered to exhibitors in the annexes and separate buildings being erected for special purposes (Harper's Weekly, May 27, 1882).

Lieutenant Governor H.A.W. Tabor (inset) served as president of the association that oversaw this ambitious industrial exposition. (*Harper's Weekly*, May 27, 1882)(*The Colorado Graphic*, February 18, 1888)

Beyond Denver

The heart and soul of Colorado has always resided in the land: majestic mountains, lush alpine parks, rushing streams, rugged mesas dotted with piñon pine. By 1883, over 1,300 miles of railroad tracks spread across Colorado like a many-tentacled monster — opening over 90,000 square miles of Colorado land for settlement and development. Men like William J. Palmer (inset), creator of the Denver and Rio Grande Railway, spearheaded this era of progress.

If drawn in proportion to its eventual impact, the small puffing train in this dark illustration would dominate the landscape. (Crofutt, 1881) (Crofutt, 1881)

Visual delights

Beyond Denver, visual delights awaited train passengers and crews alike. Here a small steam engine is shown *rolling down Clear Creek Cañon.* (Crofutt, 1881) (Crofutt, 1881)

A great resort in summer for pic-nic parties

Beaver Brook Station [above] — *Jefferson county, is situated at the junctions of small creek, called Beaver Brook with Clear Creek, in Clear Creek Cañon, on the line of the Colorado Division Union Pacific Railway, twenty-two miles west from Denver, fare $1.50. It is a great resort in summer for pic-nic parties; the scenery is very grand and beautiful* (Crofutt, 1881). (Crofutt, 1881)

Beyond recognition of its own mother — on the high line road between Black Hawk and Central City

A few more revolutions of the wheels, and the train stops at the end of the road, at CENTRAL CITY, the county seat and chief town in Gilpin county, thirty-nine miles from Denver. Altitude, 8,516; population 2,626, all of whom are connected with the mining industry, more or less.

The mountains surrounding Central [City] and Black Hawk — when gold was first discovered in them — was covered with a dense growth of pine and spruce trees, but they are about all cut off now, and the whole mountain top and sides, with the stumps and prospect holes, present a face, 'pock-marked,' we should say, were it a child, beyond recognition of its own mother (Crofutt, 1881). (Crofutt, 1881)

Mineral Baths, Idaho Springs

*I*daho [Springs], *for its hot/cold and mineral springs — and swimming baths — has become noted as an attractive summer resort. It is claimed the waters contain rare medicinal properties, and are nearly identical in chemical ingredients and temperature, with the celebrated Carlsbad water of Germany.*

At the springs are two swimming baths, one thirty by fifty feet, five feet deep, the other twenty by forty and four feet deep, also private baths, varying in temperature from 60 to 110 deg. fahr., so arranged that the bather has full control of the temperature of the water (Crofutt, 1881). (Crofutt, 1881)

Georgetown: *One of the most enterprising towns in the mining country*

GEORGETOWN *is situated in one of the richest districts of Colorado, and is reached from Denver by the Colorado Central Narrow-gauge Railway, which makes its way along the famous Clear Creek Cañon, and is one of the triumphs of modern engineering. After following the cañon for some miles, the road forks a short distance above Beaver Brook, one branch extending to Black Hawk and Central [City], and the other to Georgetown. Georgetown lies in a beautiful valley, and is one of the most enterprising towns in the mining country. Above Georgetown, Green Lake (top) was one of the most charming little resorts in Colorado (Crofutt, 1881). (Crofutt, 1881) (Frank Leslie's Illustrated Newspaper, May 5, 1883)*

A Sure Preventative

For those people in the region who became ill, Georgetown's *The Colorado Miner* (January 4, 1872) carried an ad for *THE CELEBRATED HOME STOMACH BITTERS: A SURE PREVENTATIVE for Fever and Ague, Intermittents, Billiousness, and all disorders arising from Miasmatic causes.*

Gulch Mining, Near Breckenridge

County seat [Breckenridge] of Summit county, received a town organization in May, 1880, and the census taken soon after gave a population of 1,628, which, at the close of the year, had nearly doubled; and is still rapidly increasing. It is situated on the Blue River, on the western slope of the 'Snowy Range,' eighteen miles southeast from Como, and 106 miles west from Denver. Load mines are counted by thousands in the vicinity, and large numbers of mines are producing good milling and smelting ores — the number, too numerous to mention (Crofutt, 1881). (Crofutt, 1881)

The most delightful drives and rambles

The scenery viewed from Colorado Springs is exceedingly grand. To the west 'Pike's Peak' rises full in view, from base to summit; altitude 14,336 feet, or 6,308 feet higher than the city. In the vicinity are some of the most delightful drives and rambles: Manitou, five miles; Garden of the Gods, three and one-half miles; Cheyenne Cañon, five miles; Summit of 'Pike's Peak,' fifteen miles, etc., etc. (Crofutt, 1881)

Trains heading south from Denver passed through Palmer Lake (top) on the way to Colorado Springs (bottom). (Ingersoll, 1885) (Crofutt, 1881)

A sort of gigantic peep-show in pantomime

Then there is . . . the Garden of the Gods, hidden behind those garish walls of red and yellow sandstone, so stark and out of place in the soberly-toned landscape that they travesty nature, converting the whole picture into a theatrical scene, and a highly spectacular one at that. Passing behind these sensational walls, one is not surprised to find a sort of gigantic peep-show in pantomime. The solid rocks have gone masquerading in every sort of absurd costume and character (Ingersoll, 1885). (Ingersoll, 1885) (Scribner's Monthly, August 1876)

Two views of the springs and the cliff house at Manitou

In 1876 an artist drew the illustration on the left with the man bending over to drink from the spring. Nine years later a similar view (below) reveals the addition of handrails on the bridge and an ornate cupola. These improvements were in response to the increasing number of tourists who flocked to mineral springs throughout Colorado in the 1880s and 1890s. (*Scribner's Monthly*, August 1876) (Ingersoll, 1885)

With mines came railroads

In 1891 Bob Womack, a young cowboy, found a promising gold vein west of Manitou. He sold his claim for $500. It subsequently produced over $5,000,000. Womack died a pauper, knowing he had discovered the new bonanza of Cripple Creek. Soon Cripple Creek, its population soaring to over 40,000 people, had its own railroad. Ornate vignettes on The Cripple Creek Central Railway Company are shown above. (Stock certificate: Author's collection)

In the Lobby of the Palace Hotel, Cripple Creek Colorado

To the Cripple Creek gold fields all eyes in the State are now turned for prosperity. Its location is directly behind Pike's Peak . . . . The gold fields of Cripple Creek cover an area of twelve miles, embracing half a dozen towns or suburbs radiating from the main town with its wounded name (Harpers Weekly, January 6, 1894). (Harper's Weekly, January 6, 1894)

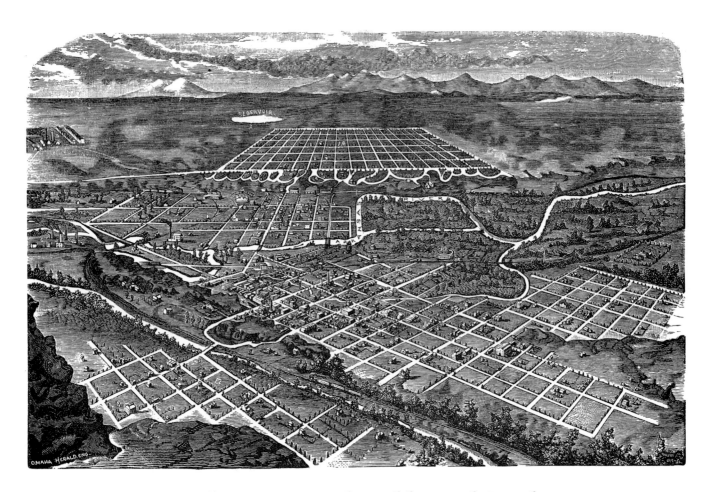

Bird's Eye View of Pueblo, and South and East Pueblo

Population of Pueblo and South Pueblo is 4,760. The business of the city is, to a great extent, connected with the mining business to the west and south — San Juan, Leadville, and the Cimarron regions. Agriculture — along the Arkansas river and the adjacent streams — is very profitable, as the yield per acre of all kinds of small grains and vegetables, is abundant; but above all others, stock-raising is the most extensive (Crofutt, 1881). (Crofutt, 1881)

Royal Gorge of the Arkansas

*D*own *this gorge rushed the accumulated waters of the ages, which, together with the erosion of centuries, have weathered the soft corners and washed away much of the loose materials, leaving rocks, rocks of every shape, form and dimensions, rocks with huge domes, towers and pinnacles, sharp corners and hollow recesses; rocks over 2,000 feet in height — standing perpendicular — with projecting spurs, almost locking the inter-locking from opposite sides. We say, imagine all these things, and you will then only have a faint conception of the 'Royal Gorge' of the Grand Cañon of the Arkansas.*

So narrow was the Cañon, in places, that the [rail] road bed had to be suspended over the river, an illustration of which will be found above (Crofutt, 1881). (Crofutt, 1881)

The ride over the mountain is exhilarating and romantic

In southern Colorado trains chug over Raton Pass near the old Sante Fe Trail. *We give on this page an illustration of the 'switchback' near Trinidad, Colorado, by which the Raton Mountains are now crossed into New Mexico. Trinidad is the southernmost town of Colorado, and the entrepot for Territory named . . . . The ride over the mountain is exhilarating and romantic, and all the more for the spice of danger there is in it: for the misplacement of a rail by half an inch, or the slipping of a brake, would hurl train and passengers hundreds of feet below (Frank Leslie's Illustrated Newspaper, August 23, 1879).* (Frank Leslie's Illustrated Newspaper, August 23, 1879)

Trip to Aspen *abounds in interest for the tourist*

The trip from Salida to Aspen abounds in interest for the tourist, it leads one through a most varied country, and presents to the inspection of the traveler almost every variety of industry, from the agriculture and stock raising of the Arkansas and Eagle River Valleys to the gold and silver mining of Leadville and Aspen, and it may be said, in passing, that Leadville and Aspen are the two greatest mining camps in the world and well worthy of a visit (Wood, 1889). (Both from Wood, 1889)

FOR BOYS AND GIRLS.

[Entered according to Act of Congress, in the year 1893, by JAMES ELVERSON, in the Office of the Librarian of Congress, at Washington, D. C.]

The *most excellent society* of Aspen

It is a town of beautiful homes, and has most excellent society. All the principal religious denominations have suitable houses of worship, and the public schools are of an excellent order. The hotels are good, there is a fine opera house, and the town is supplied with pure water from Castle Creek. An electric light plant illuminates the principal places of business as well as the streets. The climate is delicious and especially beneficial in all pulmonary complaints. Aspen is a garden town, and displays many beautiful lawns, sprinkled and beautified by flowers (Wood, 1889).

Adolescents in Aspen and throughout Colorado could subscribe to *Golden Days for Boys and Girls* among numerous other illustrated journals. Serial adventure stories featuring exotic characters and images thrilled ardent young readers. (*Golden Days,* April 1, 1893)

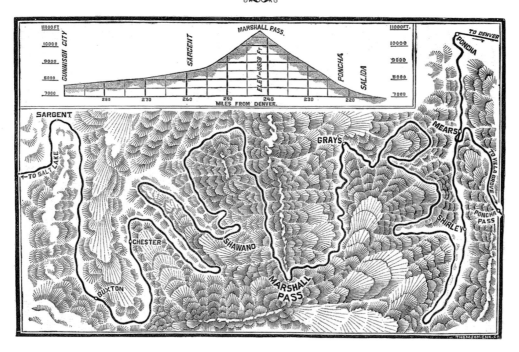

A view of the Sangre De Cristo Range from Marshall Pass

Marshall Pass Station is directly on the summit of the pass, and the track is enclosed by a large snow shed. Fine views can be obtained, however, from the loop holes or from either end of the shed. The elevation is 10,852 feet above sea level . . . as the train rolls swiftly on, a backward glance gives the traveler a comprehensive idea of the vast heights overcome in the passage (Wood, 1889). (Both from Wood, 1889)

Wagon Wheel Gap — *it has no peer in any land*

Rio Grande county, is one of the most charming summer resorts in Colorado, and taking it in all its varied attractions, it has no peer in any land. Here are located Hot Sulphur Springs of remarkable medicinal properties. The mountain scenery is grand and beautiful in the extreme. Game, such as deer, bear, elk, grouse, quail, etc., are abundant in the hills, and speckled trout in the streams, which, together with the most healthful climate, add greatly to the pleasure of a season's sojourn and rambles at Wagon Wheel Gap (Crofutt, 1881). (Crofutt, 1881)

Beyond the railroads — *Packing Cord-Wood Over the Rocky Mountains*

All high-country mines did not conveniently line the railroad tracks in the 1880s or the 1890s. Often located miles from the nearest railroad station or terminus of the track, mine owners needed to pack in tons of supplies and pack out tons of ore. Poorly treated beasts of burden (above) carried most of the load.

Far from the thriving metropolises on the eastern slope of Colorado, a few rich ore discoveries, incredibly, were still made in the early 1890s. (*Harper's Weekly,* January 7, 1888)

MINING CAMP ON THE RANGE ABOVE CREEDE.

Mining Camp on the Range above Creede

The town of Creede is in what is known as the King Solomon district, it is 320 miles from Denver, and lies directly in the pathway on the Great Divide. Why it was not discovered sooner, why, indeed, there is one square foot of land in Colorado containing silver not yet discovered, is something which the Eastern mind cannot grasp . . . . The shaft of the Last Chance Mine is at the top of the Bachelor Mountain, and one has to climb and slip for an hour and a half to reach it (Harper's Weekly, April 9, 1892). (Both from Harper's Weekly, April 9, 1892)

HOW LAND IS CLAIMED FOR BUILDING—PLANKS NAILED TOGETHER AND RESTING ON FOUR STUMPS.

Debatable Ground — A Warning to Trespassers

Near Creede a wooden billboard proclaimed (*Harper's Weekly,* April 9, 1892):

> **NOTICE**
> THIS LAND EITHER BELONGS TO R H -SATRE WHO HAS LOCATED IT
> WITH VALENTINE SCRIP OR TO THE STATE OF COLORADO. IN EITHER
> CASE YOU ARE TRESPASSING — CAN NOT POSSIBLY GAIN
> ANYTHING BY SQUATTING UPON IT. THE — MATTER WILL PROBABLY
> BE SETTLED IN 30 DAYS, AT WHICH TIME, YOU CAN PURCHASE LOTS
> AND GET A TITLE FOR PARTICULARS CALL ON   J.W. SMITH

Illustrated magazines brought the world to miners

No matter how remote the mining camps or mines, illustrated magazines still managed to find their way, albeit often after several months, into miners' hands. Picture weary miners late in the evening huddled next to a heating stove in a crude log cabin far above Creede or any remote mining camp. Imagine what they thought and what they said while viewing *The Bridal Dress of Princess Louise Margaret of Prussia, Duchess of Connaught* [above], or a *Dance Before The King of The Sofas in West Africa* [opposite page]. (*Frank Leslie's Illustrated Newspaper*, April 12, 1879, and March 1, 1894)

The prettiest mountain town in Colorado?

Ouray is — what shall I say? The prettiest mountain town in Colorado? That wouldn't do. A dozen other places would deny it, and the cynics who never saw anything different from a rough camp of cabins in some quartz gulch, would sneer that this is faint praise. Yet that it is among the most attractive in situation, in climate, in appearance, and in the society it affords, there can be no doubt. There are few western villages that can boast so much civilization (Ingersoll, 1885). (Ingersoll, 1885)

San Juan country — nature at its best

With snowcapped mountains caressing azure skies, alpine lakes swarming with trout, and turquoise rivers churning through deep rock canyons, the San Juan country in southwestern Colorado is nature at its best. Numerous illustrators and photographers wanted to make the San Juans their home. Some did. (Ingersoll, 1885) (Crofutt, 1881)

Adventures in the San Juans

San Juan mining towns like Ouray, Silverton, Durango, Telluride, Ophir, and Rico served as mining centers during the 1880s and 1890s. Above, an illustrator sketched various mining-related activities that occurred in remote regions above the towns. (*Harper's Weekly,* June 9, 1883)

Beautiful but brutal winters

On December 23, 1883, a mail carrier (inset) disappeared while attempting to deliver Christmas letters from Silverton to Ophir. They found his body in August, 1885.

Snowstorms reeked havoc upon the railroads in the San Juans and throughout Colorado. On January 24, 1885, the illustration shown here appeared in *Harper's Weekly: The gorge of the Rio de las Animas, in Southwestern Colorado, is every winter the scene of gigantic snow-slides, which sometimes delay traffic on the Denver and Rio Grande Railroad for many days. The slide illustrated* [right] ... *was fifty-seven feet deep, and occurred last winter.*

MARY·IRVIN·WRIGHT

The price of progress

It is easy to be the judge and jury of events in Colorado during the latter half of the nineteenth century. There was, however, a steep price paid for the "progress" continually championed by Americans, including influential illustrators and writers. Humans, wildlife, and the environment all suffered.

No humans suffered more terribly than the Indians. In 1890 the slaughter of over 200 Indian men, women, and children at Wounded Knee (above) in Dakota Territory has come to symbolize — to most Coloradans and Americans — the terrible price paid by those who stood in the way of one culture's concept of progress. (Mooney, 1892)

Jennie Sword, survivor of Wounded Knee

A baby girl of only three or four months was found under the snow, carefully wrapped up in a shawl, beside her dead mother, whose body was pierced by two bullets. On her head was a little cap of buckskin, upon which the American flag was embroidered in bright beadwork. She had lived through all the exposure, being only slightly frozen, and soon recovered after being brought in to the agency . . . [where] she was adopted . . . and was baptized under the name of Marguerite (Mooney, 1892). (Mooney, 1892)

What the Indian wants is simply one white man in the whole white race... who will not habitually lie to him

In 1892 Frederic Remington painted the above scene and made the following observations: *Not long ago the press despatches [sic] said that shyster lawyers in the Indian Territory were making legal raids on the Cheyennes. The Indians now have their lands in severalty, and a new assortment of trouble and care with them. The famine, the small pox, the pneumonia, the strong-water, and the Texas cowboy had nearly done for them; by now the frontier lawyer gets in his talons, and the end is nigh .... What the Indian wants is simply one white man in the whole white race who can say to him, 'you can do this,' or 'you can do that,' and who will not habitually lie to him* (Harper's Weekly, July 9, 1892). (*Harper's Weekly*, July 9, 1892)

FREDERIC REMINGTON

More "have-nots" than "haves"

During the latter half of the nineteenth century, no matter whether gold, silver, coal or whatever the substance wrested from the earth, only a relatively few people profited handsomely. Those few were the mine owners, mainly eastern industrialists and bankers. Thousands of miners in Colorado labored under slave-like conditions with abysmal pay (perhaps $3.00 at day). Owners lounged in the Brown Palace Hotel in Denver and took extended European vacations.

Seven days a week miners faced the specter of injury and death from unsafe and unhealthy working conditions. Major catastrophes happened as well: *THE awful disaster at the Colorado Coal and Iron Company's mine at Crested Butte . . . Out of sixty-seven men who went down to work that morning, only ten escaped with their lives; all the others were either killed* [opposite page] *on the spot or overpowered by the deadly gases while fleeing from the mine . . . . The mine is said to have always been considered dangerous* (*Harper's Weekly,* February 16, 1884).

Indeed, by the end of the nineteenth century, most mining towns in Colorado grieved over their own mining disasters, yet more were to come. (Both from *Harper's Weekly,* February 16, 1884)

Deadly labor disputes

In July 1893, as if the appalling pay and hazardous conditions in the mines were not bad enough (intermittent miners' strikes had failed miserably), the government withdrew its price supports for silver. Specifically, the United States repealed the Sherman Silver Purchase Act sending devastating economic ripples throughout the West. Within weeks Colorado banks closed, smelters and most silver mines shut down, jobs were lost, and real estate values tumbled. The danger of widespread hunger prompted the organization of relief committees in mining camps. Bread lines were established in Denver for the destitute.

For the next few years the owners who could afford to keep their mines (mostly gold) open had a glut of labor. Wages dropped even further. Finally, the miners had had enough. Around the turn of the twentieth century violent miners' strikes spread throughout Colorado. Several mining towns experienced near anarchy when mine owners brought in replacements (derisively dubbed "scabs") for the striking miners. Colorado governors called out the National Guard to quell the violence in Leadville (shown on opposite page in 1896), Cripple Creek, Colorado City, Telluride, Trinidad, and others. Marshall Law became the norm. In the end, the beleaguered miners had neither enough money nor clout to sustain the strikes. They went back to work under the same conditions and for the same miserable pay. (*Harper's Weekly*, December 12, 1896)

It is almost a pity that Glenwood Springs is now so famous

Despite its troubled end to the nineteenth century, Colorado knew it was something special — a place few could ultimately resist. To wit, a turn-of-the-century reporter for *Harper's Weekly* pined: *If there is in all the world a resort like Glenwood Springs in Colorado, it is modestly hiding its fame in some foreign corner. The peculiar attraction at this new rendezvous in the heart of the Rockies is an open-air hot-water swimming-pool, in which one may bathe just as delightfully when the thermometer is at the freezing point as one does at Narrgansett Pier on the hottest summer day . . . [the pool] is covered by nothing but the blue sky, and surrounded or enclosed only my Dame Nature's breath-the atmosphere . . . It is almost a pity that Glenwood Springs is now so famous.*

As we begin the twenty-first century, it surely is a pity that all Colorado remains so famous. We are in jeopardy of seriously compromising the pristine environment that made this region so enchanting in the first place. We must find a balance between population growth and preservation of our greatest asset: the environment. Enough has already been lost. (*Harper's Weekly*, March 17, 1894)

Amundson, M. A. (1994: Fall). "Pen Sketches of Promise: The Western Drawings of Merritt Dana Houghton," *Montana: The Magazine of Western History,* 54 - 65.

Bartlett, R. A. (1962). *Great Surveys of the American West.* Norman, Oklahoma: University of Oklahoma Press.

Bird, I. L. (1960 edition). *A Lady's Life in the Rocky Mountains.* Norman, Oklahoma: University of Oklahoma Press.

Black Elk Speaks: Being the Life Story of a Holy Man of the Oglala Sioux (as told through John G. Neihardt). (1932: 1995 reprint). Lincoln, Nebraska: University of Nebraska Press.

Blaine, J. G. (1886). *Twenty Years of Congress: From Lincoln to Garfield.* Volume II. Norwich, Connecticut: The Henry Bill Publishing Company.

Busch, P. (1976). *Colorado Sketchbook.* Denver, Colorado: Century One Press.

Buys, C. J. (1986). "Accounts of the Battle at Milk Creek: Implications for Historical Accuracy." *Essays and Monographs in Colorado History,* 4, 59 - 80.

Buys, C. J. (1986). "Power in the Mountains: Lucien Nunn Catapults the San Juans into the Age of Electricity." *Colorado Heritage,* 4, 25 - 37.

Buys, C. J. (1993). "Fort Crawford: A Symbol of Transition." *Journal of the Western Slope,* 8 (2), 1 - 29.

Buys, C. J. (1997). *Historic Leadville in Rare Photographs and Drawings.* Ouray, Colorado: Western Reflections, Inc.

Buys, C. J. (1997: Summer). "Of Frozen Fire Hydrants and 'Drunkin Sons of a Bitches,' Early Leadville's Volunteer Firemen." *Colorado Heritage,* 2 - 15.

Buys, C. J. (1999). *Historic Telluride in Rare Photographs.* Ouray, Colorado: Western Reflections, Inc.

Buys, C. J. (1998: Summer). "Henry M. Teller: Colorado's 'Silver Senator,'" *Colorado Heritage,* 29 - 36.

Crofutt, G. A. (1881). *Crofutt's Grip-Sack Guide of Colorado.* Omaha, Nebraska: Overland Publishing, Co.

Crofutt, G. A. (1885). *Crofutt's Grip-Sack Guide of Colorado.* Omaha, Nebraska: Overland Publishing, Co.

Denver Tribune (selected issues from 1880 through 1884). Denver, Colorado.

Dill, R. G. (1881). "History of Lake County" in *History of the Arkansas Valley, Colorado.* Chicago, Illinois: Baskin and Co.

Dyer, Rev. J. L. (1890). *The Snow-Shoe Itinerant.* Cincinnati, Ohio: Cranston & Stowe.

Firemen's Advocate (selected issues from 1854). Boston, Massachusetts.

Frank Leslie's Illustrated Newspaper (selected issues from 1879 through 1894). New York, New York.

Golden Days for Boys and Girls (selected issues from 1893). Philadelphia, Pennsylvania.

Grafton, J. (1992). *The American West in the Nineteenth Century.* Mineola, New York: Dover Publications, Inc.

Gunnison Review-Press (selected issues from 1884). Gunnison, Colorado.

Hafen, L. (editor). (1965 - 1972). *The Mountain Men and The Fur Traders of the Far West.* Glendale, California: A. H. Clarke, Co.

Hafen, L. and Hafen, A. (1948). *Colorado: A Story of the State and Its People.* Denver, Colorado: Old West Publishing Company.

Hall, F. (1889 - 1895). *History of the State of Colorado.* Volumes 1 - 4. Chicago, Illinois: The Blakely Printing Company.

Hanaford, P. A. (1883). *Daughters of America, or Women of the Century.* Augusta, Maine: True and Company.

Harper's New Monthly Magazine (selected issues from 1880). New York, New York .

Harper's Weekly (selected issues from 1859 through 1892). New York, New York .

Hayden, F. V. (1871). *Preliminary Report of the United States Geological Survey of Wyoming and Portions of Contiguous Territories.* Washington D. C.: Government Printing Office.

Hine, R. V. (1981). *In the Shadow of Fremont: Edward Kern and the Art of American Explorations, 1845 - 1860.* Norman, Oklahoma: University of Oklahoma Press.

Ingersoll, E. (1885). *The Crest of the Continent.* Chicago, Illinois: R. R. Donnelley & Sons.

Lavender, D. (1954). *Bent's Fort.* Garden City, New York: Doubleday and Company, Inc.

Mathews, A. E. (1866). *Pencil Sketches of Colorado.* Denver, Colorado.

Miller, M. E. (1997). *Hollow Victory: The White River Expedition of 1879 and the Battle of Milk Creek.* Niwot, Colorado: University of Colorado Press.

Mooney, J. (1896: 1973 reprint). *The Ghost Dance Religion and the Sioux Outbreak of 1890.* (From the Fourteenth Annual Report of the Bureau of American Ethnology, 1892 - 1893.) Glorieta, New Mexico: The Rio Grande Press, Inc.

Mountain and Plain (selected issues from 1911). Denver, Colorado.

National Republican: Senatorial Edition (1886). Washington, D. C.

Pierce, R. V. (1875: 2nd edition). *The People's Common Sense Medical Adviser in Plain English; or, Medicine Simplified.* Buffalo, New York: World's Dispensary Printing-Office and Bindary.

Reyher, K. (1998). *Antoine Robidoux and Fort Uncompahgre.* Ouray, Colorado: Western Reflections, Inc.

Rocky Mountain News (selected issues from 1896). Denver, Colorado.

Roosevelt, T. (1913). *An Autobiography.* New York, New York: The Macmillan Company.

Russell, O. (Haines, A. L., editor) (1965). *Journal of a Trapper: 1834 - 1843.* Lincoln, Nebraska: University of Nebraska Press.

Saltiel, E. H. and Barnett, G. (1868: 1975 facsimile edition). *History and Business Directory of Cheyenne and Guide to the Mining Regions of The Rocky Mountains.* New Haven, Connecticut: Yale University Library.

Scribner's Monthly (selected issues from 1876). New York, New York.

Senate Executive Document No. 78. (1855, 1856). "Reports of Explorations and Surveys to Ascertain the Most Practical and Economical Route for a Railroad from the Mississippi River to the Pacific Ocean (1853 - 4)." Volumes II and IV. Prepared by the Secretary of War. Washington, D. C.: Beverly Tucker, Printer.

Smith, D. A. (1992). *Rocky Mountain West: Colorado, Wyoming, & Montana, 1859 - 1915.* Albuquerque, New Mexico: University of New Mexico Press.

Stockades, Strikers, Bathtubs, and Other Facts (1998). Arizona State Parks: Fort Verde Historic State Park.

St. Louis Globe-Democrat (selected issues from 1896). St. Louis, Missouri.

Summerhays, M. (1911: 1979 reprint). *Vanished Arizona.* Lincoln, Nebraska: University of Nebraska Press.

Taft, R. (1953). *Artists and Illustrators of the Old West.* New York, New York: Scribner.

Telluride and San Miguel County, Colorado. (1894). Denver, Colorado: The Publishers Press Room Company (Telluride Board of Trade).

The Colorado Graphic (selected issues from 1888).

The Colorado Miner (selected issues from 1879). Georgetown, Colorado.

The Daily Chronicle (selected issues from 1879). Leadville, Colorado.

The Daily Colorado Tribune (selected issues from 1867). Denver, Colorado.

The Denver Daily Tribune (selected issues from 1876). Denver, Colorado.

The Illustrated London News (selected issues from 1881). London, England.

The Rocky Mountain Presbyterian (selected issues from 1876). Denver, Colorado.

Unrau, W. E. (1979). *Tending the Talking Wire: A Buck Soldier's View of Indian Country , 1863 - 1866.* Salt Lake City, Utah: University of Utah Press.

Wallihan, S. S. and Bigney, T. O. (1870). *The Rocky Mountain Directory and Colorado Gazetteer for 1871.* Denver, Colorado: S. S. Wallihan & Company.

Westermeier, C. P. (1970). *Colorado's First Portrait Scenes by Early Artists.* Albuquerque, New Mexico: University of New Mexico Press.

Wharton, J. E. (1866: 1909 facsimile edition). *History of The City of Denver from Its Earliest Settlement to the Present Time.* Denver, Colorado: Byers & Daily.

Williams' Tourists' Guide and Map of The San Juan Mines of Colorado (1877). (Publisher unknown).

Wood, S. (1889). *Over the Range to the Golden Gate.* Chicago, Illinois: R. R. Donnelly & Sons.